THERE WAS BLOOD
ON THE SNOW

THERE WAS BLOOD ON THE SNOW

DAVID HUNTER

RUTLEDGE HILL PRESS
Nashville, Tennessee

Published in Nashville, Tennessee, by Rutledge Hill Press, 513 Third Avenue South, Nashville, Tennessee 37210

Typography by Bailey Typography, Nashville, Tennessee

Library of Congress Cataloging-in-Publication Data

Hunter, David, 1947–
    There was blood on the snow / David Hunter.
      p. cm.
    ISBN 1-55853-131-9
    1. Law enforcement—Tennessee—Knoxville—Case studies. 2. Crime—Tennessee—Knoxville—Case studies. 3. Hunter, David, 1947–
4. Police—Tennessee—Knoxville—Biography. I. Title.
HV7914.H86 1991
363.2'092—dc20
    [B]   91-32749
                                                     CIP

Printed in the United States of America
1 2 3 4 5 6 7 8—97 96 95 94 93 92 91

I Dedicate This Book to My Children
—Kristi, Elaine, and Paris—
Who Have Often Made Life Difficult,
But at the Same Time Gave it Meaning

Contents

Introduction

SUCCESS MAY BE the gravest danger an artist faces. Poverty and rejection are much easier to overcome; those dangers are clearly visible and forthright. Celebrity status is quicksand, treacherous and lethal.

The business of an artist is to create and define, to open windows on the universe through which others may peer as he struggles to make sense of his own existence. In the purest sense, art must be created as simply and unconsciously as a spider spins silken webs—and for the same reason—because it is impossible *not* to do it.

In the final pages of my first published book, *The Moon Is Always Full*, I spoke of seeking simplicity as a police officer on the streets and roads of Knox County, Tennessee, just as Thoreau sought simplicity by a pond called Walden. A woman at a book-signing in Birmingham told me that it was a "pretentious statement." She didn't stay long enough to be questioned, but it was obvious that I had somehow hit a nerve.

The woman, I suspect, came from the ivy-covered halls of academia where my work, for the most part, has been ignored. After all, I don't belong to the club. My single excursion into the world of higher education ended rather badly.

A course called "Becoming a Productive Writer" (or some similar title) was offered by a community college in Charlotte, North Carolina, while I was living there in the early 1970s. The teacher, whose name has vanished from my memory, was teaching from a self-printed pamphlet he had written. In everyday life he was a school teacher.

Five minutes into the class, it became obvious to me that he had no idea of the process involved in selling a manuscript to a real-life editor. To save time, I asked him for his credits.

He haughtily explained to me that he did not write "commercial garbage" and that his art was of the kind done for the sake of art. I understood him perfectly; he had never sold anything. I departed without further ado. By that time in my life I had done a lot of writing for the sake of art and wanted not only to be read but to make a little money for my efforts.

Thereafter, I avoided academic authors for the same reason that George Fox, founder of the Quakers, avoided the clergymen of his day—they had nothing to teach me.

I sat down and wrote. The payoff—becoming a published author—was a long time in coming, but it finally arrived. Suddenly my name was in the local papers, the Associated Press wrote about me, and I began to hear from people in faraway places.

It was heady stuff after all the years I had devoted to my art without external rewards. Invitations began to come in, and I accepted them all indiscriminately: literary clubs, lawyers' groups, Kiwanis, Lions, The Exchange Club, Legal Secretaries, and many I don't remember.

I had become an investigator just before my first book was bought, and each passing week took me further from the world of the street cop that I described in my writing.

Not only was I becoming distant from my roots, but somehow, between television interviews and speaking engagements, I was spending more time talking about being a cop and talking about being a writer than I spent doing either of them. The celebrity was taking over, interfering with the artist.

It was my wife, Cheryl, who finally brought it into perspective. "I think you should go back to patrol," she told me. I must have stared at her in shock. Everyone (who watches television) knows that a cop's wife wants him out of harm's way, behind a desk if possible.

"You're not happy," she said. "You don't talk about your work anymore, and you dread every shift."

Cheryl was absolutely right. Less than a month later I was back in my blue suit, a patrolman again at the age of forty-three, a time when most cops are looking for office jobs.

The patrol job took me back to night shifts and away from the afternoon speaking engagements. My writing picked up immediately because I was back to the fundamentals, both in my art and in my police work. I was back out there with the warriors, far removed from silk ties, luncheons, and seminars.

I saw a lot of new faces on patrol. Many of them were strange to me. It was awkward for a little while, working with people who knew me through my books but whom I had never met. Soon, though, I was just another cop to them.

That's the way I like it: simple, uncomplicated, intense, elemental.

As I have written twice already, these stories are true, with names changed and dates moved around to protect privacy. There are composites for the sake of brevity, but the stories are real. Most take place in Knoxville, but only incidentally. The world of cops, wherever they are, is a miniature model of the human condition.

Welcome back to my world.

1

There Was Blood on the Snow

"THE SEVERAL INCHES of snow had left a blanket over the county, and I thought it was going to be a slow day," Dale Gourley told me. Gourley's beat is Blount County at the foothills of the Great Smoky Mountains, which rise majestically against the skyline. In many ways, Blount County is a typical East Tennessee county.

On one side smokestacks rising from the Aluminum Companies of America plants mark an industrial area. On the other side is God's country, or at least the place where He spends His off-duty time. The sight of the Smoky Mountains is enough to bring a lump to the throat of any mountain-bred native.

It had made sense for Dale to expect a slow day. Although it snows in East Tennessee, it does not snow often, certainly not enough to justify large expenditures for expensive snow moving equipment. Residents of Blount County and the surrounding area basically come to a halt when it snows.

Except for police officers and other emergency service people, the natives don't get enough practice to become adept at driving over snow-covered asphalt and concrete.

After a mad rush for home at the first sign of snow, life becomes pretty quiet.

"I was on the New Walland Highway when the dispatcher called for my unit. I was given a call that would change my life forever," Dale later recalled.

The dispatcher had informed him of a sledding accident with injuries involved. He was told that an ambulance had already been dispatched.

Thirteen miles from the accident, Gourley moved as quickly as he could with only snow tires for traction. Off and on the road and sideways much of the time, he made the trip in eighteen minutes.

In a large city with several precincts, an eighteen-minute response time would be unacceptable. In rural East Tennessee across snow-covered roads, it was an impressive response time.

Dale stayed on well-traveled roads as much as possible, but the final approach was over a road that was not heavily traveled, even in good weather. As he crested the final hill, he gasped and dropped into a lower gear as the car gained momentum. There were marks of a sled on the snow-covered pavement in front of him.

"I traveled the same path the sledders had taken," Dale told me.

As he slid to a halt, he became aware that the sled tracks all ended on an embankment that the riders had been using to stop their momentum—all except one set of tracks that continued out into the middle of an intersection. High embankments on all sides had blocked the view from both directions. Apparently, the sledders had expected no traffic. They were wrong.

As Dale entered the intersection, the horror unfolded. Two small children, attended by two men, lay in one lane. A third and older child lay on the other side of the road. He had turned painfully on his side so that he could see his younger sister and brother.

"I'm all right," the oldest boy said despite a badly broken arm as Gourley approached. "Help them!"

"I turned to the nearest child," Gourley said, "and saw a man trying to perform CPR, or what he thought was CPR." Kneeling beside the child, Dale told the man to stop pushing on the boy's stomach.

"I checked for a pulse and noticed how cold to the touch he was. Then I saw the dark-colored blood coming from his ears and mouth."

Knowing that the boy probably had been killed on impact, Dale turned to assist with the other child. At the same time, the man who had been trying to blow the breath of life into his five-year-old daughter turned to face the officer.

"Isn't there anything you can do for my son?"

"No," Gourley said, dropping his head.

"What do you think?" the man asked desperately, indicating his daughter.

"There was no way I could tell him she was dead, too. I told him to keep working on her, and he went back to work without hesitation. The breaths of air he gave made little gurgling sounds as the lifeless lungs tried to expand."

As the ambulance pulled up, Dale saw a man standing with his hands covering his face. He was the driver of the truck that had struck the children. Gourley took his statement as emergency technicians loaded the two lifeless bodies and the one living child.

The driver, his truck loaded down with firewood, had not seen the sled moving into his path until a second before impact. On dry pavement, he might have stopped. Of course, on dry pavement the sled would not have crossed his path.

He braked, but there was no traction on the snow. The five thousand-pound truck bore down on the three children and pushed the sled down the road, crushing them under its wheels as it ground to a halt.

"Why?" the anguished driver kept asking.

There was no answer. Perhaps the driver knew it even as he asked.

Armed with the details, Officer Dale Gourley turned to mark the spots where the children had come to rest. Marking the scene is an important task because fatal accidents require precise diagrams.

Gourley paused, standing quietly. The moment haunts him still.

"As I started to mark the final resting places, I saw that it had already been done. There was blood on the snow where each of them had come to rest."

That scene burned itself into Dale Gourley's mind. No longer were the snow-covered hills an excuse for snowballs, snow cream, and sledding. Winter sports had lost their magic. The snow reminded him of only one thing—the blood of children splashed crimson against a blinding white background.

Twelve years later, Dale Gourley read my first book, *The Moon Is Always Full*. The chapter "Haunted Streets," in which I spoke of seeing the ghosts of victims of violence on my beat, had dredged up memories of that long-ago day when a young patrolman answered an accident call on a snowy morning.

Dale called me, but he was unable to tell his story because the wound was still too sore. I suggested that if he wrote everything down, it might be therapeutic.

A few days later, the account arrived in the mail. It was on computer paper in no-nonsense black and white. The story was so vivid that I could see the blood in the snow and knew there was steam rising from the spots marked in red that morning.

A short time later, Dale called. I knew his healing had begun with the telling of the story.

"Hunter," he said, "yesterday I told my oldest daughter that when it snows, we're going sledding."

He paused and swallowed hard, almost suppressing the

sob working at the back of his throat. "I told her we'd go to a safe place . . . but we're going."

He *should* go sledding with his children. The joy of life should not be stolen by memories of the past. The ghosts fade slowly, but I believe that Gourley will be able to file away—with other horrors—that memory of blood on the snow.

— 2 —

The One-Hundred-and-Twenty-Dollar Girl

"I DIDN'T BUY ANY whiskey, but I had an offer of sex for hire," the Alcoholic Beverage Commission Officer said with a laugh.

"Describe the girl," I said tiredly.

"They called her Cindy. She looks like she might have been a real doll at one time, but hard living has left its mark. Dark hair, petite, and with a beauty mark on her upper lip."

He was right. Cindy (not her real name) had been a living, breathing doll when she hit the strip joints at the age of eighteen. Four years later, she looked thirty. My mission with the Alcoholic Beverage Commission had been to find illegal whiskey. Cindy had complicated my work, though. She had made it appear that I was not doing my job, which at the time was beverage control, overseeing the behavior of bar owners and their employees.

"I don't guess you'd prosecute her, would you?" I asked hopefully.

"I can't afford to blow my cover," he answered.

"Right," I replied. "I'll deal with her tomorrow."

On the way home that morning, I remembered the first time I had met Cindy. I first noticed her as I was doing a walk-through at a now extinct nude bar on Clinton Highway while I was on patrol. She caught my attention for two reasons: I had never seen her, and she was beautiful, both unusual attributes in the grubby strip joints along the highway.

She was finishing her routine as I walked into the bar. Her eyes were focused ahead as the crowd went wild. I realized instantly that she was new to the business. Eye contact with the crowd is something an exotic dancer must develop.

I was standing by the bar at the back of the stage when she stepped down, holding flimsy panties and a transparent bra. Spotting my uniform, her eyes flickered to my face and she blushed. Blushing was an ability I knew she would quickly lose.

"Does your mother know you're out tonight?" I asked.

She turned her back to me and quickly stepped into the panties and bra. "What . . . what do you mean?"

"I mean, find some identification and bring it to me. I don't think you're old enough to be in here."

The bar owner scowled from across the room as she went to find her purse, but he said nothing. He was perfectly aware that one of my fantasies was to catch him doing something wrong and parade him out of the bar in handcuffs, preferably before a television crew.

"Here," she said, returning with a driver's license and birth certificate. "I've been eighteen years old for *three* months."

"I still want to know if your mother knows you're here."

She blushed again. "No! And it's none of her business."

"I hope to be as wise at sixty as you are at eighteen," I replied, handing back her papers. "Why don't you go home, get back in school, and get a part-time job at McDonald's. You're in over your head on this highway."

"I can't make the kind of money selling hamburgers that I'll make here. I've just started, and I've already made over a hundred in tips—just tonight." She stared at me defiantly, her black eyes flashing.

"It's your life, but if you stay out here, you'll be selling more than a dance pretty soon."

"I'd never do that. I'm not *that* kind of girl!!"

I shrugged and left. Watching lovely young women go down the tubes had become a common occurrence on my North Knoxville beat. From experience, I had learned that most of the dancers, at least those who confided in me, had been sexually abused as children. As time passed, I learned that Cindy was no exception.

It was only a short time until I encountered her again. The night manager of a rundown, fleabag motel near the bar where she worked called in a disturbance. As I wheeled in, I saw Cindy in a doorway, naked from the waist up, trying to break away from a burly and balding man in his fifties. Two bright red welts were obvious across her back.

The man did not see me until I was almost on him. He tried to slam the door, but I kicked it open and stepped in.

"Back off!" I snapped at him.

"This is private," the man whined.

"It became *public* when I got here, Mister. Put your clothes on, Cindy, and wait outside." She complied, sobbing. When she was out of the room, I had a private chat with the big-bellied man, explaining in graphic detail how I felt about his activities and suggesting serious repercussions if he ever showed up on my beat again.

"It wasn't what it looked like, Officer Hunter," Cindy told me, wiping tears from her cheeks as we talked later. "I just came by his room to have a drink, that's all. It's not what you think. I wouldn't do *that* for money." Somehow it seemed important to her that I believe her. It was as if she could remain innocent as long as I believed her.

"Of course not," I replied.

On the way home, she offered to repay my kindness in the only way she knew how. She seemed hurt but not offended as I explained to her why I wasn't interested. It was not my first such conversation with dancers on that high-way, nor the last.

After that night, I numbered Cindy among my network of informants, without which a street cop makes few cases. Four years later, she put me into a situation where I had no choice but to take action against her.

The music assaulted my ears and the doorman nodded as I walked into the so-called "lounge." In reality it was a beer joint with naked girls as a draw, even more dingy and dirty than the bar in which I first saw Cindy. Beer was drunk straight from the can at three times the retail price on store shelves. The flashing lights around the stage winked through the haze of cigarette smoke hanging in the air.

It was my second walk-through that night. Two of my friends, Bob Wooldridge of the Knoxville Police Department and Jim Watson of the sheriff's department, were helping me out. Bob, wearing a convention name tag that showed him to be a sales representative from Philadelphia, was playing the part of an out-of-towner, with Jim as his tour guide. It was an easy part for Bob. He is from Philadelphia and sounds like it.

Our prearranged signal was for Bob to stroke his mustache if he had been solicited. Unknown to me, a problem had come up after my first walk-through. A petty criminal had recognized Bob and was telling everyone, including Cindy, in a whispered voice that he was a cop.

She may not have believed the man. More likely, however, was that she was playing games with Bob. Like other citizens, the misconceptions that prostitutes have about the law could fill a book. One myth among prostitutes is that if the girl names an unusual price, the judge and jury won't believe the undercover officer.

The price that Cindy decided on was a hundred and twenty dollars—not fifty, not one hundred, but the unusual sum of one hundred and twenty dollars. She was also laboring under another misconception, a common one. Cindy believed that she had to graphically describe what she would do for the one hundred and twenty dollars. In reality, it is enough for the girl to communicate that she is selling sex for money, regardless of how the deal is made.

What she told Bob was that for one hundred and twenty dollars "expense money" she would meet him in his hotel room for "a little fun." It was enough. When I walked through, Bob stroked his mustache. I nodded my head and called for back-up. At the time, Mike Upchurch was still running Clinton Highway as a patrol officer. He arrived in minutes.

Bob and Jim took Cindy, naked and protesting, from the stage, told her to dress, then cuffed her. A drunk who became too curious and got in the way was arrested by Upchurch for being publicly drunk.

Jim and Bob arrived at the jail ahead of me and were in the process of booking Cindy when I arrived. She looked up hopefully as I came down the hallway.

"Officer Hunter is here now," she said smugly. "He'll straighten this out."

"Hunter is the one who set you up," Bob said, concentrating on his paperwork.

She sat, as if stunned, staring at me like an injured child. There seemed to be nothing for me to say, so I left.

Cindy was in for a hard time. When she went to work the next night, laughing co-workers handed her a shirt that said "120 DOLLAR GIRL."

"Call Cindy," the note said. I carried it back to my office, puzzled. A year had passed since the arrest, and I had not heard from her. As a matter of routine, I hooked up my tape recorder to the phone and dialed.

"Hello." Her tongue was thick.

"Cindy, this is David Hunter. What can I do for you?" I was pretty sure of what she wanted to discuss. I had brought charges against the bar, and they were trying to clean up their act before the hearing. Her conviction for prostitution would not look good for an employee.

"I wanted to tell you. I'm leavin' town. They've fired me at the bar, but I had somethin' to say to you."

"What did you want to tell me, Cindy?"

"I didn't . . . I never offered to sell my body to that man you sent in," she sobbed. "I don't know why he lied to you, but he did. You know . . . you *know* I'm not that kind of girl."

"Are you taking some kind of drug, Cindy? Are you all right?"

"Just a little Valium an' beer. I'm givin' up dancin'. I have a job as a waitress in Atlanta." Her words slurred out. "I wanted to set the record straight before I lef', though. I didn't offer to sell my body to that man." She began to cry softly.

"I believe you, Cindy," I said gently, not bothering to tell her that she was talking about one of my closest friends or that I knew she had pled guilty to the charge.

"Thank you." She hung up, and I didn't see her for two years. Her former boss told me that she had gone to work in Atlanta, not as a waitress but as a massage parlor worker.

It would be nice if I could say Cindy married a nice man and became a housewife somewhere in middle America with a house full of kids. If this were fiction or a movie script, it would have a happy ending. It didn't happen that way, though: it seldom does. A novel or a movie ends at some point, but a real life goes on.

The next time I saw her, there were needle marks up and down her arm and sores on her mouth. She didn't appear in the least embarrassed to be strutting across the stage stark naked.

I would imagine, though I haven't asked her, that she would no longer be embarrassed to admit that she is a prostitute.

Whatever remnant of self-respect that once made her

deny it has been dead a while now. Her eyes are as tired and vacant as all the other dancers on the highway.

One hundred and twenty dollars is a lot more than anyone would be willing to pay for her now.

3

Lily of the Field

"**J**UST THIRTY-FIVE MORE days," the thin, blond man said, slopping warm, soapy water on the kitchen tiles. "Then I start over. No more jail, no more sleepin' with a buncha hardtail men."

"Good for you," I replied. At the time, a green jailer with only a few days under my belt, I still had a great deal of confidence in the ability of human beings to change. Gilbert (the name I'll use) was the first inmate to convince me he had seen the error of his ways—but not the last.

"Yep, I've learned my lesson *this* time. I'll walk the straight and narrow. I've got a good woman waitin' on me, and she's found me a job. It ain't much, but it's a start."

"How many times have you been in?" I asked.

"Six times, but it's the last." He wrung the mop out and began to remove the excess water from the floor.

Gilbert was twenty-six. I discovered this when I was booking him back in later. His background was middle-class, and he had graduated from high school. For some reason, though, somewhere along the way, Gilbert had decided that almost anything was better than working for a living. During our first conversation, I knew none of this.

"So you're getting married, huh?"

"Yep. I'm marryin' one of my counselors. She's a fine girl. Owns her own home and everything."

I was a little surprised to hear that a professional counselor was marrying one of her charges. My naiveté on the subject did not last long, though. One of the hazards faced by women who deal with prisoners is the love affair that often springs up.

Why this happens I don't know. Perhaps men in jail touch a woman's maternal instinct or the messianic hope in each of us that we can lead others to salvation. In Tennessee a few years ago, a lawyer helped her imprisoned lover escape, tossing her career down the drain.

Every morning, Gilbert counted down another day until at last his parole date arrived. Just after shift change that Friday afternoon, I helped him carry his meager belongings to the front door. I shook his hand.

"Good luck, Gilbert."

"Thanks, officer." He went through the outer door. He was met by a shy-looking young woman. She was not pretty, but she was not unpleasant either. About thirty, she was medium-size, with her brown hair clipped short.

They were driving out of state to get married but would skip the honeymoon, Gilbert had told me. The following Monday he would start his job as a kitchen helper, and she would go back to counseling inmates.

"Go down front and let Gilbert and his parole officer in," the sergeant said, handing me a parole violation warrant. "He's surrendering."

"Is this Gilbert the kitchen trustee?" I asked.

"One and the same," the sergeant replied.

"The same Gilbert who got out two weeks ago? The same Gilbert who counted the days until his release? The same Gilbert who married the counselor?"

"That's him," the sergeant said.

"Doesn't seem possible he could have violated his parole so quickly."

"He got married Saturday," the sergeant said. "On Tuesday he took his wife's new car, her silver, all her jewelry, and her bank card. He wrecked the car, sold her valuables, and spent all the money in her cash account."

I walked down to the front and let Gilbert and his parole officer in. Nodding to the officer, I spoke to Gilbert.

"You didn't stay out long, did you?"

"No," he smiled, "but I had one hell of a time while I was out, though!"

I waited for the punchline, but it did not come. Gilbert went back to the pen, but he returned less than a year later, once more eligible for parole.

"Sixty-one days," Gilbert said, as he sat in the trustee tank polishing a pair of shoes. Trustees often made extra spending money by spit-shining shoes for the jail officers. "And I'll be back on the streets."

"Are you going to stay out longer than you did the last time?"

"Who knows?" Gilbert said philosophically. "I had so much fun the last time, I probably would have died if it had gone on much longer."

"Gilbert, excuse me for prying, but you've had eight days of freedom in the last three years—that I know of. You've made no profit from it. Why do you keep it up? You can do better."

"Actually, Hunter, I've been on the streets less than a year total since I was eighteen."

"Doesn't that seem like a waste?"

He wet a cotton ball and rubbed short, brisk circles on the toe of the shoe he was polishing.

"Do you like the job you're doin' right now, Hunter?"

"No," I replied, "but it's the means to an end. I'll be a cop in a little while."

"You come in every day to a job you hate, Hunter. I've never had to do that."

"Yeah, that's true, Gilbert, but eventually I'll be out doing what I want."

"You'll die of stress, Hunter. Or you'll crack up because you let things bother you. You think things matter, but they don't. You ever read the Bible?"

"Yes, Gilbert. What does *that* have to do with this?"

"Well, Jesus said not to worry because our needs will be provided. He said there wasn't anything more beautiful than a lily of the field, and lilies don't do anything but grow and look pretty. I'm like a lily of the field. I don't work, and my needs are provided anyway."

He took a final look at the shoe, put it down, and picked up another. He rubbed paste on his fingers and went to work.

"Gilbert," I said, desperately looking for common ground, "have you ever been raped? I never have."

"Sure," he said, "a buncha times when I first went up. It happens to ever'body. It's like an initiation. It happens 'til you have friends to protect you."

"It doesn't bother you?"

"Well, I didn't *like* it, but it's the way things are. You'd probably kill yourself if it happened to you. That's the difference between us. I know it makes no difference at all. It's just somethin' that happened one time."

"Just out of curiosity, what do you have planned when you get out in sixty days?"

"I'm goin' to my wife's place."

"The social worker?"

"Naw. My *real* wife. We've been married since before I went to jail the first time."

"What does she do for a living?"

"She's a whore, but right now I think she's got some old man keepin' her up. She said I could move in when I got out though."

"I see." Sighing in frustration, I started down the walk.

"No, you don't," Gilbert said. "You woulda stayed with

the social worker. She woulda sent you to college, and you could have *both* died of boredom together."

"Baker 10 and Baker 14, disturbance in progress. . . ."

I jotted down the address and headed toward it. The morning shift had been slow, and I was glad for the break in the boredom. Mike Upchurch and I arrived at the driveway simultaneously, coming from opposite sides of the beat. We crunched up the rocky driveway and got out. It was a big white house—rundown and tattered—that had been divided into apartments.

The front door of a basement apartment opened, and a woman of indeterminate age (between thirty and fifty) opened the door. She was thin, with a front tooth missing. Her hair was bleached platinum, but an inch or so of black had grown out at the roots. It was cut in a "Cleopatra" style.

"What's the problem?" Upchurch asked in his rolling drawl.

"It's my husband. He's destroyin' all my valuables."

"Is he armed?" I asked.

"Yeah. With a kitchen knife. He's been cuttin' up all my clothes he can git his hands on. I want him out of here."

We stepped through the door, hands on our weapons. A small, emaciated man sat at a red Formica kitchen table. He was in his sixties, at least. His hair was gray and looked like he might have started wearing it shoulder length about the time the hippies were walking around Haight-Asbury. His eyes loomed huge behind his thick glasses.

"Stand up," Upchurch ordered him.

"No! That ain't my husband. That's Charlie. My husband run up the stairs." She pointed at a doorway.

"Where do the stairs go?" I asked.

"Nowhere," she replied. "They're closed off."

Drawing my weapon, I cautiously opened the door and

pointed my flashlight up the stairs. A man squatted at the top, staring back at me. It was Gilbert.

"Don't shoot," he said. "I throwed the knife down at the bottom of the stairs."

"Come on down, Gilbert," I told him.

"All right," Mike Upchurch said, "let's get this sorted out. You tell your story first, lady. Everyone else be quiet."

"Well, Gilbert got outta the pen last Friday. Me and Charlie let him come here—like we've always done. But Gilbert ain't happy with that. He wants to take *liberties* with me."

"What relationship is Charlie?" I asked.

"He's my fee-ancy," she said, holding up her hand to show us a cheap, gaudy ring.

"Let me get this straight," Upchurch said. "You're married to Gilbert, Charlie is your fiancé, and you all live here together?"

"That's right," she said primly, "and Gilbert has been tryin' to take liberties with me—right in front of my fee-ancy."

"I screwed her all weekend," Gilbert said, "at five bucks a toss—in front of *him*. She went right along until I run out of money."

"Was not in front of Charlie! He turned his back ever' time, didn't ya, honey? Don't you try to make me out as some kind of kinky pervert, Gilbert!"

"Enough!" I said. "Do you have anywhere to go, Gilbert? You have to leave here or go to jail."

"I kin go to the mission," he replied.

"Fine, let's get moving," I retorted.

"Ninety-four days, Hunter."

I turned from the coffee urn and saw Gilbert. In the jail looking for some records on a violator I was tracking, I had walked over to the kitchen to take a break. It had been nearly three years since I had seen him, nine since the first

time I met him. There were a few more jailhouse tattoos on
his arms, but little else about him had changed.

"Now, why am I not surprised to see you, Gilbert?"

"We have to stop meetin' like this," he snickered.

"How's your wife, Gilbert?"

"She's fine. We'll be celebratin' our seventeenth anniversary this year. It's comin' up right after I get out."

"She still with Charlie?" I asked.

"No. Ole Charlie died not long ago. I hated to hear it. He
was a nice old man. Never beat on my wife."

"What's your wife doing now?" I took a sip of my coffee.

"Turnin' tricks across from the bus station," he said matter of factly. "She's puttin' a few bucks aside. We'll probably take a trip to Myrtle Beach when I get out this time—
for our anniversary."

"I don't guess it would make any difference if I pointed
out that you could be free all the time if you wanted to."

"No, I guess not. On the outside I'd have to work a menial job to survive."

"You're working a menial job *now*," I said.

"No, I'm not. There's a hundred guys here who'd like to
be a trustee. But everybody knows I won't run off. I'm one
of the top dogs here."

I laughed out loud and shook my head.

"You think it's funny, Hunter. Have you checked your
blood pressure lately?"

"Yeah, Gilbert, and it's high. But I haven't spent a single
day of my life locked up."

"I know," he answered, "so you really only got somebody's word that it's *bad*. I never sow, but I always reap. I've
never been hungry, and I ain't done a day's work on the
outside since I got out of high school. I'm like a lily of the
field."

"Gilbert, I'll see you next time." I threw my plastic cup
into the garbage.

"Try to relax, Hunter. Stress will kill you."

He's right about the stress, but I am depending on the
wonders of modern medical science to see me through.

— 4 —

Ivory Towers

"**D**ISTURBANCE IN PROGRESS," the dispatcher said, then gave me the address of a well-known strip joint on 25W. A customer, the dispatcher said, was involved in a dispute over money and was standing outside, cursing and threatening the owner.

Wheeling in, I saw the man. He was visibly swaying, shaking his fist at the owner who was standing in the door. The man turned and looked at me with a bleary expression.

"I want him arrested," the man said, staggering toward me, pointing at the manager. The man was in his mid-thirties. He was wearing an expensive suit and was neatly trimmed—not the usual Clinton Highway bar patron.

"For what?" I asked.

"He's got girls dancin' *naked* in there. I happen to know it's illegal for girls to dance naked."

"What's the problem here?" I asked the owner.

"He bought a table dance, then wouldn't pay for it. When the girl insisted, he got real abusive. I told him to calm down or I'd call the law. He *dared* me to do it."

A "table dance" is a dance performed at the customer's table. As long as there is no physical contact between the dancers and the customers, and as long as the dancer does not give an "obscene" performance (in the opinion of the attorney general's office), there is nothing a Knox County officer can do.

"Arrest him," the man said. "I *know* the law."

"If that's the case, then you know it's against the law to drink yourself into a state where you're a danger to yourself and against the law to breach the peace. You're under arrest for being drunk and disorderly. Put your hands on the side of my cruiser and spread your legs."

He ranted all the way to the Knox County jail.

"Are you tellin' me that indecent exposure's not illegal? It's all right to dance naked?"

"Depends," I said. "If they do it downtown during rush hour, I'll arrest them, but the charge will be disorderly conduct, not indecent exposure."

"That's ridiculous." He slurred his words. "Totally ridiculous."

"Once upon a time indecent exposure was 'common law,' never written down but *understood*. Urinating in public was enough for indecent exposure," I explained. "Then the legislature decided to clarify it. Now we have to prove that the exposure was for the purpose of offending or provoking sexual stimulation. Try to prove *that*," I said.

"I can't believe it," the man whined somewhat redundantly. "A good citizen calls to report a crime and you arrest *him*."

"Well, between me and you, I suspect that you never would have called if they hadn't upset you. And you weren't arrested for calling, but for drinking yourself nearly comatose."

"Anyway, maybe it's time you came down from your middle-class ivory tower to find out what actually goes on out here in the real world."

Every night there are shootings, rapes, stabbings, robberies, and burglaries, as well as every other category of crime imaginable. Only the most flagrant ever get into the newspaper.

John Q. Citizen pays little attention unless it is *his* house that is burglarized or a member of *his* family that is assaulted. Crime is something to be watched on television— entertainment, not reality.

Unfortunately, there are people other than average citizens who maintain themselves in insulated environments long after they should have learned better. One such category comes under the heading of "social workers."

One of the worst insults a cop can throw at another is to call him a "social worker." It probably works the other way, too. Many social workers regard cops as Neanderthals, insensitive and unresponsive to human pain.

The ongoing argument is silly. Society needs the skills of both professions. There are good social workers and incompetent social workers, just as there are good and incompetent cops. Silly or not, the feud persists and is helped little by those members of both professions who insist on viewing everyone else as inferior.

I was dispatched one night to meet with two social workers at a small market on 25W regarding "confidential information." For obvious reasons, I will not identify them.

"I'm Officer Hunter. What can I do for you?"

One was about twenty-five, had auburn hair, smiled as I approached, and was extremely pretty. The other strongly resembled a giant bullfrog in expression and build, with none of a frog's warmth, though, I must add. She did not appear much older than her partner.

"That strip bar right up the street," she snapped without preliminaries, "is not supposed to allow juvenile girls to dance."

"May I inquire where you received your information?" I asked. Every girl dancing on Clinton Highway at that time had proper identification. It was one of the things I personally monitored.

"No, you may *not* ask. My sources are confidential!"

Her answer made things crystal clear. She was acting on an anonymous complaint. There were two nude bars along that stretch of highway at the time. They took turns snitching on each other—anonymously.

"Follow me," I said.

Minutes later, we were at the front door. The bouncer snapped the electronic lock as I approached and looked questioningly at the two women.

"Social workers," I said.

The owner of the bar came across the crowded room, a pained expression on his face. It was seldom that my presence heralded good news for him.

"Is there somethin' wrong, officer?"

"These ladies are social workers. They have a complaint that you are employing underage girls."

"You checked all my girls this week."

"I know, but they want to check again."

"We can go to the back room," he said with a sigh.

"No. We can stand right here and check the identification," I said. "There's no need to interrupt business. Just bring the girls one at a time and have them show their papers."

I turned and looked at the two women. The bullfrog's mouth was open as she stared red-faced at the platform, where a totally naked girl of twenty or so was advancing in a strut, lips pouting, displaying her most intimate shadows to the screaming, shouting crowd. The one with the auburn hair merely looked fascinated, staring first at the dancer, then at the men who were all waving money at her.

One by one the dancers produced identification. The bullfrog read each card, nose in the air. Her partner watched the show intently. Having checked all the girls, we left the bar.

"This is *disgusting*," the bullfrog said. "They *must* be breaking the law."

"I agree it's disgusting," I said cheerfully, "but the attorney general has the final say. A cop can't even sign an obscenity warrant until the attorney general's office rules on the matter and countersigns."

"How much do those girls make?" the auburn-haired one asked me.

"On this highway, fifty to a hundred dollars a night. In the really plush clubs down west, they can make several hundred a night."

"I will most certainly file—" the bullfrog began. She was interrupted by her partner.

"I'm in the wrong business," the social worker said.

"Ma'am," I said gallantly, "it's a filthy business, but I'm sure you'd be a crowd pleaser."

"Let's go!" the bullfrog snorted. Her partner gave me a dimpled smile as they drove away.

"We have to go to a house right up the road here."

It was my second encounter with the bullfrog. As before, she had jumped in without preliminaries.

"Are you going to the Halston [pseudonym] residence?"

"Yes, why do you ask?"

"I have to advise you that it's not safe to go there."

"I *know* that. My supervisor says the police report called it a volatile situation. That's the *only* reason I asked for an officer. The sheriff's department took a battered teenage girl out of there yesterday. I have to interview the parents in order to determine what to do with the child."

"I'm the officer who wrote the report. The father of the battered girl is off the deep end. I backed the girl out of that yard with my hand on my weapon."

"If he's so dangerous, why didn't you *arrest* him?" She glared at me triumphantly, as if she had just scored a point.

"Because at the time, I had no legal reason to arrest him. [There was no domestic violence law in Tennessee then.] The girl was battered, but not sufficiently to classify it as a felony. The girl was my primary concern."

"Well, I have to go interview him, and you've been ordered to assist me." She turned to her car, as if the matter was settled.

"*Wrong*. I'm here to evaluate the situation and see if police action is feasible. I'll go up there, then I'll decide what happens next. Stop your car behind mine. *Do not* pull into that driveway."

In the curve, just below the house we were seeking, I stopped and looked through the trees. Two cars were pulled nose to nose across the driveway. On the porch wooden chairs had been piled in front of the door.

"I'm ready," the bullfrog huffed up behind me, pad and pencil in hand.

"I'm not going up there, and I'd strongly advise that you don't either."

"And *why not?*"

"The man in that house has gone into a siege mentality. See how the driveway's blocked? See the chairs in front of the door? Any approach to that house becomes a kill zone. His daughter told me that he has sporting rifles inside."

"Can't you call the SWAT team?" she asked.

"Lady, I have no warrant or other legal reason to go up there! He does not *have* to talk to you. I'd suggest you call his wife. She's the only one who can deal with him right now."

"Well, I'm going."

As she started toward the driveway, I took my shotgun from the cruiser and racked in a round. She stopped and turned.

"I thought you weren't going?"

"I'm not, but if he kills you in my presence, I'll be obligated to take him out, if I can. Of course, if I can't get him, his wife will be a hostage."

"Oh, *all right!* I'll call them, but rest assured there'll be a full report made on this incident and your lack of cooperation."

"I wouldn't have it any other way," I replied.

"It was unreal," the narcotics officer said, laughing cynically. "This college girl and her boyfriend are out looking for some cocaine. They drive right over to the combat zone in her new Mercedes, pull up to the curb, stop the first black guy that comes by, and ask where they can score the toot.

"The guy reaches in, takes her keys, rips off her necklace and watch, then demands her boyfriend's wallet—which he hands over with no argument.

"He stands there long enough to go through the wallet, then throws it and the keys in the front seat and *thanks* them before he leaves.

"The college girl goes to a telephone, all indignant, and calls us. I asked her what the hell she expected drivin' into the most dangerous neighborhood in the city.

"She tells me that she wants 'police protection.' I told her that if rich kids like her would stop financing drug dealers, we wouldn't have to spend all our time chasin' them. She'll probably call in a complaint on me."

Ivory towers, where the inhabitants know nothing of the real world. They drive through during the day, perhaps noting the poverty in an offhand manner but not really grasping that there are people out there who do not see the world the way prosperous, middle and upper America sees it.

They have no conception of insanity, drug induced or otherwise. Nor do they understand that when they hit the streets of the underworld they become fair game for those who cannot be seen from the elevated heights of middle- and upper-class America.

Oh yes, we do have social classes in America. And those people who have not yet seen that need to be serenaded.

"Come down, come down from your ivory towers . . . ."

—5—

Anything But the Truth

"**U**NIT 10, CAN YOU come to my location?"

"Ten-four," I replied. I had been listening with interest as the patrol officer answered a call to check a 10–90 [suspicious] car parked in a driveway. It was only a couple of doors down from my house. There is seldom a police call in my neighborhood.

Rolling in a few minutes later, I saw Benita Thompson talking to a woman who appeared extremely agitated.

"I figured you'd want to know about this, since you live so close," Benita said. Benita (B. J. to her friends) is a veteran patrol officer. We go back a few years.

"I appreciate it. What do you have?"

"Really, just a car parked where it shouldn't be," she shrugged. Citizens tend to get excited easily.

"This is *twice* now," the complainant said. She was a woman in her mid-thirties, well-groomed and definitely upset.

"It's probably a boyfriend parking here, then walking to his lover's house. I'm sure Officer Thompson told you that."

"Yes, but I'm having trouble with my husband's family

over the will. They didn't think I should have inherited because we're divorced. *You* remember."

The complainant's ex-husband had committed suicide, leaving everything to his ex-wife. The sheriff's department had been forced to intervene that same day as family members attempted to load up items from the house.

"I remember. Have you been having problems with the family, or do you recognize this car?"

"No," she shivered, "but I'm still worried about it."

"It's blocking your driveway," Officer Thompson said. "You can have it towed at the owner's expense if you want to."

"No, I don't want to make them any angrier—if it's them."

"All right," Benita said. "We'll put a watch on the house."

Before we left, I jotted down the tag number. The next morning, I went to records.

"Find out who this car belongs to, then check the name and address for a driver's license."

A driver's license gives a date of birth, description, and address. With that information, you can check for a police record. The name was not in our records, nor was he wanted anywhere—at least, not under that name. I filed the information and waited. All things come to him who waits.

The car appeared twice more but was parked on the street, not in a driveway. When I finally got my information, it did not come from police files.

"Is this Officer Hunter?"

"Yes, who is this?" I did not recognize the voice, and officers zealously guard their phone numbers. If the public gets them, they have to be changed.

"One of your neighbors [she named her] works with me. She didn't think you would mind if she gave your number to me. I'll see that nobody else gets it."

"All right, what can I do for you?" I did mind, but there was nothing I could do about it. When a cop's phone number leaks to the neighborhood, people call him instead of the department.

"I know all about that car that's been parked near your house."

"Tell me about it."

"My sister-in-law and brother live in your subdivision. That car belongs to her boyfriend. My brother caught them having an affair once before."

"That's pretty much what I figured."

"Something needs to be done," she said.

"Well, we may find adultery distasteful, but it's not a crime. At least it hasn't been enforced in years, if it's still on the books."

"They have a baby. My mother and I are afraid that she's leaving the baby alone. My brother works at night."

"Apparently, she's not going anywhere," I said. "The car is parked in the neighborhood. Her boyfriend is probably walking to the house."

"We're worried. I was hoping you could help."

"I'd help if I could, but this is not a police matter. If you think a baby's being neglected, you need to take this matter up with your brother."

"Thanks anyway," she said, "but he believes everything his wife tells him, no matter how ridiculous."

"Or *pretends* to believe," I replied. "I've seen that before."

In the records section I checked my mailbox. You never know what to expect. Usually it's a stack of reports—offenses, arrests, and memos. It was part of my job to sift all daily reports, looking for criminal intelligence and indiscretions at bars.

"David?"

"Yes?" I turned and saw that it was a teleserve clerk who

answers all non-emergency calls coming in to the sheriff's department.

"Why are you in uniform?" she asked.

"I've been to the funeral home, standing honor guard for Smitty," I replied. She had never seen me in the blue suit. I had become an investigator before she arrived.

"Building security called. There's a man out front demanding to see an investigator about a case of blackmail. You're the only officer here tonight."

"Tell him to come back tomorrow. Blackmail is not an emergency, and it needs to be handled by the detective bureau, not beverage control."

"He's creating a scene. Demands to see an officer *now*."

"All right," I said with a sigh. "Tell him I'll stop on the way to my office and talk to him. I'll do a preliminary report and put it in the detectives' box for follow-up tomorrow."

The young man, age twenty-five or so, was standing in front of the security office. Mechanic or electrician was my first impression. Short, wiry, with hair clipped by a barber, not a stylist. He was dressed in blue jeans and a casual plaid shirt.

Behind him was a young woman with long, honey blond hair and glasses. The glasses were just thick enough to distort her eyes when she looked directly at you. Her face was streaked with tears.

"I want a warrant," he said without preliminaries, "for blackmail. I want him arrested tonight!"

I gave him the unemotional, hard stare that I reserve for people who are rude or pushy.

"Come to my office, and we'll discuss it."

"There's nothin' to discuss. You'll arrest him tonight."

"Before we go any further," I stopped and turned, "let's have an understanding. *You* do not give orders here. I will listen to your problem. Whether or not *anyone* is arrested will be up to a judge. Do you understand that?"

He nodded assent, his indignation subsiding a degree or two.

In the office, I dug out an offense report and a legal pad to take notes. "All right, let's hear the story."

"This man that my wife used to work for has been blackmailing her to have sex with him! I *know* blackmail is against the law." He looked triumphant.

"Sir, if you will *calmly* give me the information. Let's just start with your name and address."

As soon as he reeled off the address, I knew it was a continuation of the suspicious vehicle call. The young man was my neighbor.

"My wife used to work with this guy. He bothered her so much that I made her quit. A few weeks ago, he called her and said if she didn't meet him for sex, he'd kill me and the baby."

The woman began to sob as he got to this part of the story.

"To your knowledge, has this man ever killed anyone before?" I already knew the answer to that question, having checked the man's background.

"What does that have to do with anything? He *said* he'd do it this time. That's all that counts."

"No, I'm afraid not. The judge is going to ask these same questions—if you try for a warrant. Has this man, to your knowledge, ma'am, ever killed anyone?"

"I'll answer the questions. My wife is too upset."

"No, your wife will answer the questions. She is the alleged victim." The man set his lips in a grim line.

"N . . . n . . . not that I know of," she sobbed.

"Then why did you think he might carry out his threat?"

"I . . . I . . . don't know. I just *did*. It was awful. He made me sleep with him." She sobbed uncontrollably, watching her husband from the corner of her eye.

"My wife ain't on trial!" the man growled. "There's a detective down the road from me. I'll go see if I can't get a little help from *him*." The man stood. "Come on, honey!"

"*I'm* the officer who lives down the road from you. Sit down! I want your wife to go outside and close the door so we can talk." She left, sobbing dramatically, without waiting to be told a second time.

"If you don't do something, I'll take matters into my own hands." The man folded his arms and glared at me.

"Don't come on to me with the macho threats, Mister. Because any threat you make in my presence may come back to haunt you."

"All right. I just want to know what you intend to do about this blackmail."

"Was he blackmailing your wife the last time you caught them together?"

"Don't you accuse my wife—" He stood up belligerently.

"Sit down, *now*!" He dropped into the chair, eyes downcast.

"Well?" I asked.

"No, but it was just a mistake on her part. Everybody makes mistakes. I know she wouldn't do it again . . . not unless she was forced into it." His expression cried out for belief. His macho image had evaporated.

"Now." I was also quieter, the truth having been arrived at. "This is painful, I know. The fact is, though, this has been going on for some time now. Your wife's boyfriend has been parking down the road and walking to your house.

"If you want a report, I'll write it. But there are two things you should know. First, it's against the law to knowingly file a false police report. Secondly, if I write this report, it becomes public record. The reporters won't believe your wife's story anymore than I believe it—or you believe it—but they may put it in the paper and giggle while they do it.

"Do you want me to write this report?"

"No." He would not look me in the eye.

"Then go home and try to work out your problems with a therapist or a minister. The police have crimes to work on."

He went through the door without saying anything and

motioned for his wife to follow. She looked at him, then turned to me with a hateful glance. Her husband's expression told her the charade was over.

They never came back for a warrant. Whatever story she came up with to explain her lie and her affair must have worked. He wanted to believe her and was willing to face ridicule rather than admit that his wife was unfaithful.

"Look," I said tiredly into the telephone, "if the FBI couldn't help you, there's nothing the sheriff's department can do. Besides, I've told you, the Central Intelligence Agency does not carry out operations in this country—only overseas."

Once more I was the victim of having been the only officer in the building when an unhinged party called. A homicide detective was on duty, but he was busy. The woman at the other end had insisted on any investigator. Upon answering, I had listened to a bizarre story unfold. The woman claimed her husband had been kidnapped by the CIA and forced to take part in a drug operation to capture international dealers.

It's best if cranks at the other end of a phone line are humored. Usually they are satisfied if you tell them you'll "check into it." This woman was of a different variety.

"I want you to talk to my husband. You'll believe him in person. I know the story sounds far-fetched, but it's *true*. I'm sending him down there to talk to you."

"All right," I said with resignation, looking at my watch, "but I get off at three. If he's not here before two-thirty, I'll be gone. Have him come through the front door of the City–County Building. Security can show him where my office is."

I went back to sorting reports, feeling extremely sorry for myself and all cops who have to put up with crazy people in the name of public relations. It was less than fifteen minutes before there was a rap on my door.

He was a mahogany-colored man with conservatively

clipped hair, tall and neatly dressed. *At least,* I thought, *he looks fairly sane.*

"Are you Robert Quall?"

"Yes."

"Have a seat."

I sat watching him for a moment. There was no glint in his eye, no hidden fervor. If anything, he appeared embarrassed.

"I understand you've already talked to the FBI, Mr. Quall. Is that true?"

"Naw, I just told my wife that."

"Then why didn't you just *tell* her that you talked to me instead of driving all the way down here at two in the morning?"

"'Cause she'll call to see if I've been here, and if you can't tell her what I was wearin', she'll start this up again tomorrow."

"She says you were kidnapped and forced to take part in a drug bust with CIA agents. Is that true?"

"Naw." He shook his head, smiling sheepishly.

"Then what *is* this all about?"

"I was off to Atlanta with a lady for a while."

"And you made up this story?"

"Naw, I told my wife I was out of town on an errand for my boss, but she wouldn't believe it. *Then* I made up this story."

"She didn't believe you were working, but she believed you had been kidnapped by the Central Intelligence Agency?"

"I think she *knows* better, but she *wants* to believe it. All she had to do was call my boss to see if I was workin', but she really can't prove *this* story ain't true."

"That's very astute reasoning, Mr. Quall. Now, what am I going to tell your wife when she calls back?"

"Just tell her you're passin' the information on to the right people. I think that'll do it." He stood to leave. "I'm sorry about all this, but it just got outta hand."

He was right. She did call to confirm his visit (clothes inquiry and all), and I told her the information would go to the "correct party." That was the end of the matter.

A refusal to look at the truth is fairly common. No person wants to admit that *his* child was drinking when he cracked up the car. No man or woman wants to admit that his or her spouse is unfaithful. Most of the time, self-deceit is not as extreme as in the incidents in this chapter.

Sometimes, though, people want anything *but* the truth.

—6—

Not with a Bang, But a Whimper

SEVERAL YEARS BACK, I read a book called *The Savage God* by a man named Alvarez. It dealt with suicide victims, among them the poet Sylvia Plath. It was fascinating because at the time I was going through a period of heavy depression.

Even in my blackest moment, however, suicide was never one of my options. The very idea horrified me. As the years passed and my work brought me into contact with suicide victims, the horror did not decrease. It loomed larger.

Most human beings die *fighting* for life. It is a terrifying thing to watch another human being die, something I have often witnessed as a police officer and an ambulance driver. It is not something to which you become calloused. Each death you see reminds you that one day you, too, will draw a final breath.

Life is all the more precious when at risk every day. As a result, suicide invokes terror and fear in most police officers.

What terrible thing overwhelms the most basic of desires—the drive to live, the very root of existence? "Can I fall prey to it?" you ask.

Very often the person who self-destructed gave no previous warning, leaving cops to believe that the suicidal impulse can strike without warning. It is a chilling concept to those who carry on their persons at all times—usually by departmental order—the tools of destruction.

"He was cleanin' his swimmin' pool when I left yesterday," the man said angrily of his dead brother. "Does a man who is about to kill himself clean out the swimmin' pool?"

"Yes sir," I answered. "They also wash their cars, till their gardens, talk to their friends about trivial things. Then, without warning, they kill themselves. It's hard to accept, I know, but it happens."

"Well, I don't believe it, not for a second. Not my brother! Somebody *killed* him."

Murder is easier to accept than suicide. A murder victim did not turn his back on loved ones, did not leave without explanation. There was a *reason*, a reason that everyone can understand for the murder. Not so with suicide.

He was laughing yesterday.

He talked about his vacation next week.

He had appointments in his book.

He had never seemed happier.

He killed himself.

"Something's wrong!" the man said as the officer climbed the stairs. "She was thrashing around, and now she won't answer me."

The door was locked from the inside, and it took several minutes to batter it open. Inside, even the veteran officer was shaken by what he found.

The woman lay on her back, eyes open and fixed on the next world. Beside her was a large, sharp butcher knife. She had been very nearly decapitated.

Sending the husband from the room, the officer called for an ambulance and first responder, even though he knew she was beyond help. At the same time, he surveyed the room carefully. The door was locked from the inside, as was the window. There were no hidden panels, no openings to the ceiling.

There was only a blood-spattered room and a woman with her head almost severed from her body, lying with arms and legs askew. By evidence of the blood and disarray, she had obviously taken some time to die.

The homicide investigator went over the room even more closely than the patrol officer. He examined the victim for other cuts. Almost always, a person stabbed or slashed to death has small cuts on their hands and fingers—defense wounds. There were none.

There was only the fatal gash that had nearly taken the woman's head off—in a locked room with no other entrance.

Later, under the proper light, the chemically enhanced imprint of the back of the blade across her palms emerged clearly. The test is accurate enough that a key print can be discerned on a thumb hours after the metal contacts the flesh while turning a lock.

The woman had taken the butcher knife in her hands and, gripping it by the back of the blade, had raised it to her throat and sawed it into the flesh with enough force to nearly take her head off.

In her case, death was not instantaneous. One lives until the brain dies of oxygen deprivation; one is *aware* until the blood no longer feeds the brain. She had ripped several inches into her own throat, then thrashed on the floor until she died.

Later, looking at the pictures, I shuddered. How could a human being do such a thing to herself? What pain brought on self-destruction of such a violent nature?

Had the incident occurred in previous times, her husband might have been convicted of murder by a community that never would have believed such horror possible. A community would have accepted *any* other explanation than what really happened.

If *she* could do that to herself, what about me?

Not all suicides are obvious, and not all can be ruled suicide.

Every officer has worked a fatal automobile accident in which there was absolutely no logical explanation for the crash. A perfectly good stretch of road, no mechanical problems with the vehicle, and no skidmarks—just a twisted chunk of metal with the victim wrapped inside it.

Death must be ruled accidental in such cases.

There is a case on record in Knox County, Tennessee, in which a police officer fired a shot that proved fatal to the suspect. His death, however, was ruled suicide.

After a family dispute, the man waited on the police, armed with a handgun. As the officer approached, pump shotgun at the ready, the man refused to put his pistol down.

Among the witnesses was a reporter who later wrote of the officer's attempt to get the man to drop the weapon. Finally, when the officer was too close to miss, the man raised his pistol and pointed it at the officer.

He died as a *result* of double aught buckshot penetrating his vitals. The *cause* of death, however, said medical examiner Dr. Randy Pedigo, was suicide.

A suicide usually victimizes more than one person. In that case, the officer was the second victim.

"I got a call from this little market," my brother Larry told me as he sipped his coffee, "one night when it was snowing. It came in as a 10–81 [shot(s) fired]. You know, nothing spectacular. When I got there, I saw a car parked by the building, but there didn't seem to be anything wrong.

"I went in and asked the clerk what the problem was. She said a guy had come in and asked for empty cardboard boxes. She found some for him, and he carried them out. A minute later, she heard what sounded like a shot.

"I figured it was somebody with firecrackers, but I went out to look around. Everything still looked O.K., until I noticed the steam coming up from the pavement under the front car door and the dark stain in the snow. When I got closer, I saw it was blood dripping through the crack under the door.

"I jerked out my weapon—you never know what you've got—and eased up on my toes. I still couldn't see anything, so I moved in closer. There was a man in the car with no head.

"It shook me. I called for an ambulance, even though I knew he wouldn't need one."

Larry paused, shuddered slightly, then went on.

"It was a mess. Blood poured out when the door was opened. The roof of the car was covered with bone splinters and brains. He'd put a twelve-gauge under his chin. It blew away everything except two flaps of skin on each side of his face.

"I kept looking at those cardboard boxes, though. They were in the back seat.

"This guy had gone into a store and asked for boxes. He *needed* them for something. Then he went outside, put the boxes in the back seat, got into the car, and *blew his head off!*

"What happened between the time he got the boxes and the time he got to the car? If he had left home with the intention of killing himself, why would he have gone in and asked for boxes?

"Think about it. He was going to use the boxes for *something*. What was it that happened in the few minutes between the time he asked for them and when he blew his head off?

"It's *scary*. I can tell you that," Larry said.

Some undoubtedly see suicide as high drama.

Victims jump from bridges, set themselves on fire, or hang themselves as a final statement, though often the import is lost on other people.

That people change their minds in the split second after the deed is done is indisputable. In the case of bridge jumpers, they often swim to shore and live happily ever after.

One often wonders, though, what it must feel like to change your mind, then be unable to take it back. Hanging comes to mind. Persons hanged from gallows by professional executioners usually die quickly. The drop snaps the neck, breaking the spinal cord.

Amateurs who hang themselves seldom fare so well. Death is usually by strangulation, neither quick nor romantic, as Officer Janie Grigsby found one afternoon.

"A neighbor had called in because she saw something unusual hanging from the back porch. I walked around the house, and there he was. He had been hanging for some time. In fact, if I hadn't found him when I did, he had been hanging so long that he would have probably just *slipped* through the rope.

"Another neighbor said she had seen *something* hanging from the back porch a couple of days earlier, but didn't pay any attention."

"What a way to go," I said.

Indeed.

The man had arrived at some sort of emotional apocalypse and had decided that he no longer could bear existence in this world. He would not go quietly, though. His death would be noted and dramatic. Those who neglected him would *see* what they had wrought.

Looping the cord around his neck, he had apparently walked out on the back porch, tied the cord to the railing and dropped over. It makes you wonder: Did he look around first? Did he envision the horror and shock on the faces of family and friends when they found him?

There was no excitement, though, no outcry of public

horror. He could have been a bag of garbage, a rug, or laundry hanging there for days—for all the effect he had on the neighbors.

By the time friends and family had been notified, he was out of view at the undertaker's. There was sadness, I'm sure, among friends and family.

Nothing that he had imagined, however. No sirens or flashing lights. Just a disgusted cop and ambulance attendants who, with stony distaste, handled the mess he had made.

As poet T. S. Eliot put it, "Not with a bang, but a whimper."

— 7 —

Walter Mitty Lives

"**O**N THE CAR," I said. "Do it now!"

The man was about thirty. The black Stetson hat he wore was cocked at a jaunty angle on the back of his head. In his white suit, worn with an open collar and gold chain, he would have blended in at a gathering of pimps. His alligator shoes sparkled.

In his belt I found a Browning nine-millimeter, semi-automatic pistol. Often I had lusted after such a weapon but had never been able to justify the expenditure on a cop's salary. It was, at the time, considered the Cadillac of pistols.

"You're under arrest for carrying a weapon," I told him. The "pat down," which I had begun before placing him in the cruiser for a breath test, became a search "pursuant to a legal arrest." I found some cocaine, a straw, a small mirror, and a single-edge razor blade in his vest pocket.

Cuffing him, I put him in the cruiser and called for a wrecker. I inventoried the contents of his Corvette, expecting to find a stash of drugs. The car was clean, however. Even the ashtray sparkled, although he had cigarettes in his shirt pocket. When the wrecker arrived to pull the car in, I started downtown with my prisoner.

"How much trouble am I in?"

"Well, I stopped you for erratic driving. You have alcohol on your breath, cocaine and paraphernalia in your pocket, and a nine-millimeter pistol in your belt. That all adds up to serious."

"Can you get me a blood test for drugs?" he asked.

"Why? I'm not charging you with *using* cocaine, just possession."

"I want you to know that I don't use cocaine. Without the test, you'll never believe it."

"Then why did you have it in your pocket, along with the paraphernalia to use it? You didn't have enough to be selling it."

"This is embarrassing."

"Well?"

"It impresses women at the bars I go to."

"Come on, pal. Are you trying to tell me that you purchased an illicit drug just to pick up women in bars?"

"Yes, and the same for the pistol. I've never shot it. I don't even know how to load it. It's for show. Some women are turned on when they see the gun and cocaine. They want excitement. I don't even smoke cigarettes—except for show."

Pulling to the side of the road, I picked up the nine-millimeter pistol and dropped the clip. It was empty. I peered down the barrel and saw no residue at all.

"Do you know what happens to people who make threats with empty weapons?" I asked, pulling away from the curb.

"I don't do *that*. It's just a *prop*, like the cocaine and this outfit I'm wearing. You don't think I actually dress like this do you? Nobody ever sees that weapon except the women."

"And the cop who arrests you for driving and drinking."

"I know. I shouldn't have done it. Will you get the drug test for me?"

"No, but you can still get a valid test for coke after you make bond. Bring the results, and have your lawyer talk to the attorney general—if you're telling the truth."

I booked him on the charges and ran a criminal history. His record was as clean as new snow. Most puzzling of all, he was a highly paid systems analyst for a banking chain. Apparently he made a habit of dressing like a pimp and carrying an empty nine-millimeter pistol.

The attorney general and the defense lawyer approached me in the hallway behind Sessions Court where the deals are cut before formal hearings. If even a small percent of cases went to trial, the legal system would break down.

"Did this Perkins [pseudonym] give you any problems?" the assistant attorney general asked.

"Nope, but he did register .12 percent on the breath test, and it was real cocaine and a real pistol," I replied.

"He's pleading guilty on the drunk driving," the attorney general said. "Did you check his history?"

"Yeah, he was clean."

"He's in therapy," the defense lawyer said, "dealing with his fantasies."

"Here's what they propose," the attorney general told me. "He pleads guilty and is sentenced on the drunk driving, but we'll defer sentencing on the cocaine and carrying the weapon. If no further problems, we'll wipe them at the end of a year."

"You're the boss," I said.

"Also, his lawyer has drawn up an order giving you the pistol," the attorney general said.

"*What?*"

"It's legal. He wants to be rid of the pistol—whatever we decide. He can do what he wants with it."

"It smacks of extortion," I replied. "I think I'll pass."

"It's up to you, but he wants you to have it because you treated him decently."

"No thanks," I answered, thinking of the shiny, sleek pistol with longing.

"It's up to you," the attorney general said with a shrug.

As far as I know, the systems analyst lived happily ever

after and is still designing intricate computer programs for banks. Hopefully, he had cleared *his* system of dangerous fantasies.

The Walter Mitty syndrome is not limited, however, to the affluent, as I found on Clinton Highway one night. Author James Thurber's fantasy hero turns up when you least expect him.

"He was drivin' an old red Chevy pick-up," the bar owner said. "I woulda called sooner, but I kept hopin' he'd leave without anybody gettin' hurt. We suspected as soon as we saw that silver-colored pistol in his belt that he was the one. When that ski mask and rope fell on the floor outta his pocket, we *knew*."

An armed robber, wearing a ski mask and carrying a silver-colored revolver had hit several establishments over a period of weeks. He always left his victims with hands tied behind them at the scene.

"That bandit hasn't hit the north end," I said dubiously.

"Well, I *know* it was him. If he hadn't dropped that mask and rope in front of us, I bet he would have knocked us over."

I looked at the owner, a small, wrinkled individual, with a pale complexion that seldom saw the sun. It was obvious that the possibility of having served up an armed robber was the high point of his week.

"Mike, the guy always hits clerks by themselves. It's his trademark. He wouldn't suddenly start robbing groups of people—*but*," I raised my hand to halt his protests, "I'll scour the vicinity. If I see the red truck, I'll check him out."

I drove away, intending to check the bars along 25W, but was dispatched on a domestic disturbance call, then an alarm at a warehouse. It was nearly an hour later when the dispatcher called.

"Possible 10–52 [armed robbery] suspect," she said, then gave me the location. It was another Clinton Highway bar. "The complainant says the suspect has a silver revolver in his belt and has dropped a ski mask and rope on the floor."

"Ten-four, start me a back-up." Back-up, I knew, would be coming from all over, even if I had not asked for it. Armed robbery suspects get the adrenalin flowing in cops.

Across the street from the bar, I pulled in behind a mobile home lot to wait on another car. As I waited, however, the suspect staggered from the front door. The bouncer followed and watched as he walked toward an old red pick-up truck.

I wanted no pursuit that night, so I dropped my cruiser in gear, shot across the highway and jumped out, leveling my weapon at his back.

"Police! Stop right there. Hands out to the side where I can see them."

"Don't shoot! It's a joke. It's all a joke!"

"There's nothing funny here," I said. "Lace your fingers and lock them behind your head. Drop to your knees! Good, now cross your ankles!"

"Just don't shoot. It's a joke!"

I squeezed his fingers together with my left hand, holstered my weapon, and locked the cuffs down.

"You're not very bright, are you?" I asked, pulling him to his feet and removing a pistol from the front of his belt. It was silver and looked like an old foreign-made Saturday night special. In his right jacket pocket was a black ski mask and a short length of hemp cord.

"I'm drunk," the man said, "but I ain't who you think I am."

"Oh, yeah," I put him in the back of the cruiser. "Who do I think you are?"

"You think I'm the guy who's been knockin' over convenience stores."

I watched him in the rear-view mirror. A grubby man with a two- or three-day stubble, he looked as if he had been sleeping in his truck.

"Well, the problem you now have is to convince me you're *not* the guy."

"Check out the pistol."

I opened the cylinder on the cheap revolver. It was a blank pistol, the kind they use to start races. I shrugged.

"So? The bandit hasn't *shot* anyone. He could have been carrying a blank pistol. It's still armed robbery."

"Check with the jail, they'll tell you where I've been for the last ninety days—doin' time for drunk drivin', that's where I've been."

"I'll check when we get downtown. You're still publicly drunk, whether you robbed anybody or not."

At the booking table, the grubby little man sat smoking and speaking to all the jailers with familiarity. He *had* been in jail for ninety days. He had committed none of the robberies.

"What made you pull a stupid trick like that?" I asked, moving my seat up to the booking table. "One of those Clinton Highway tush-hogs could have decided to make a citizens' arrest with a shotgun, or some rookie cop might have put you away by accident."

"I know," he said, dropping his head. "But everybody was payin' attention to me. I guess I just like attention."

"Did you go out and buy this stuff?"

"Naw. I had the blank pistol. The ski mask and a roll of rope was already in that old truck I bought. It was the ski mask that gave me the idea. I felt like somebody else while I was scarin' all them people.

"They looked at me with *respect*."

They are out there, the pretenders.

Any cop who stays on the streets long enough will meet them. Sometimes these situations don't have a happy ending. When drugs or alcohol are involved, these individuals sometimes forget that cops carry real guns and that they are only pretend adventurers, not the real thing.

Even ordinary citizens are subject to seizures of fantasy.

It chills a patrol officer to the bone when the dispatcher says that a citizen is in foot pursuit of a thief and that the citizen is armed. An armed citizen under the rush of adrenalin can be more dangerous than a criminal. He has probably never faced an armed adversary. Now he has suddenly decided to eradicate crime on his block, carrying a weapon he probably hasn't fired since he bought it and put it in the drawer beside his bed.

While I was checking on a suspicious vehicle in a rural area one night, I was shaken from my dangerous complacency as a man walked from a clump of trees in front of me. All I saw as my flashlight swept over him was the rifle. Screaming for him to drop it, I drew down and began to squeeze the trigger.

"Don't shoot!" The rifle hit the ground. "I'm on your side."

He was about my age, wearing camouflage fatigues, a headband, and military boots. Shirtless and with the carbine, he looked like a guerrilla freedom fighter. All that was missing was camouflage paint.

I chewed him out, wrecking public relations for the night. He endured silently—head down—until I had vented my anger.

"I'm sorry, Officer. I was just gonna help."

"Just be quiet and follow me. *Don't* load a round in that carbine. I still have to look for that suspicious vehicle."

The suspicious car had either left or had never been there. By the time we were finished, I had calmed down.

"I didn't mean to be so hard on you awhile ago, but you scared me. I almost shot you. Don't ever come out when you know officers are searching an area—especially not with a weapon."

"I'll know the next time. Thanks. Goodnight, Officer."

"Goodnight, Walter," I said under my breath, walking back to the cruiser.

— 8 —

The Piqued Purloiner and Other Reports

DETECTIVE CARL SEIDER is an investigator of crimes against persons, more commonly known as the homicide unit. In a large department there are people assigned exclusively to homicide. In Knox County, the homicide unit works rape, homicide, kidnappings—all "major" crimes. If there is no burglary detective in the wee hours of the morning, the homicide unit catches those also.

Seider is a thin man with short, neat hair and a slight stoop that we associate with scholars. This is fitting because Carl *is* a scholar. He holds a master's degree in criminal justice from the University of Tennessee.

He is also possessed of a wry sense of humor that is all the more devastating because he is a man of few words. To call him taciturn is like saying that anthracite coal is slightly black.

Carl Seider does not abide fools gracefully.

As part of my job, I used to sift through all reports submitted by officers. The two major reports are arrest reports and offense reports. Offense reports are classified by type so that the FBI can keep abreast of crime trends.

An assault, for instance, is classified "assault" or "aggravated assault." In the next space this will be broken down again. If it was a misdemeanor assault, it will say "simple." Thus it is classified, "assault/simple." In felony assaults, the first block will say "aggravated assault," and the next block will say "weapon/knife." Thus, the data gatherer knows how to classify it.

The first block names the crime, the second gives more detail. A burglary will be "home burglary/forced" or "business burglary/no force." A larceny will be "larceny/grand" or "larceny/petit."

You get the idea.

Sometimes, no matter how you try to break it down, there will always be situations not covered in the rule book. In such cases there is a special classification. It is simply called "miscellaneous/incident." That means a report was made, but nobody really knows why.

Irate citizens who demand a report about the neighbor's surly attitude or who want to report flying saucers end up on a report that says "miscellaneous/incident"—or in the case of the flying saucers—"miscellaneous/unidentified flying object."

When I ran across a report one morning that was marked "miscellaneous/piqued purloiner," I knew that Seider had written it. I also knew that he was smiling to himself, thinking of the supervisors and records clerks who would have to hunt down a dictionary.

A woman had broken into her boyfriend's house. She stole one item: a wedding ring that had belonged to the man's mother. The woman freely admitted that she had taken the ring because her boyfriend had been stringing her along. She said she would give it back when he was ready to make their engagement "official" by voluntarily *giving* her the ring.

Technically, a burglary and larceny had taken place. In reality, it was a domestic dispute. Carl knew there would be no prosecution. If a report was made out, however, which

said "home burglary/no force," it would become "official."
At the end of the year, when burglaries are tallied, it would
be listed on FBI statistical sheets as a burglary. Police look
bad enough without frivolous burglary reports.

Carl compromised by writing a report that essentially
meant nothing but made the complainant happy.

I understand that the purloiner and her boyfriend made
up and that she is no longer piqued.

        It was a "simple assault" report, done in Mike
Upchurch's slanted script, margin to margin across the
page. It went into detail with words to this effect:

> The victim says he has been having problems with
> woodpeckers, which are destroying his power pole. He says
> that early this morning he shot a woodpecker that was in a tree
> by his residence.
> Victim says that a few minutes later, a neighbor who lives on
> the hill above his residence knocked on the door. When the
> victim opened the door, he says his neighbor proceeded to slap
> him in the face with a dead woodpecker, while stating that the
> victim had endangered his (the neighbor's) family by shooting
> in their direction.
> The victim does not know at this time if he will prosecute.

Fortunately, the victim did not prosecute. Not only
would a judge have had difficulty keeping a straight face,
but the victim would have been forced to give testimony
under oath that he had killed a bird on the endangered species list, which would have no doubt interested the fish and
game officials.

While unusual, assaults carried out with animals as the
weapon happen. I know an officer who became a legend in
his own time when he was accused of slapping a citizen in
the face with a catfish while answering a disturbance call by
the river. He, of course, denied it. Years later, I asked him
about the truthfulness of the story.

"It was a damned lie," he said. "I didn't slap him with a catfish. It was a carp."

For sheer brevity, an officer named Claude Hall may hold the record. He turned in a report marked "animal bite/cat." The narrative said simply: "Complainant says the family cat bit her three year old son on the ear as he was choking it."

All state certified police officers in Tennessee have attended an academy, either in Tennessee or in a state recognized as meeting Tennessee's standards. They have had a minimal amount of training in state laws and in report writing. Unfortunately, not all people bonded to make arrests have attended such academies. In particular, security guards. Some are well trained, others are not.

A recent arrest report confirmed this for me. It was a case of "fondling" or "sexual battery." The security officer who made the arrest apparently did not know the law and did not bother to ask any number of officers at the jail what it was.

His perpetrator had, without warning, grabbed a female customer by the breast. The guard charged the man with "sexual abuse," which applies only to children. I was already smiling about the incorrect charge when I got to the narrative.

Either the guard was unfamiliar with anatomical terms or he did not want to appear too technical.

"While standing in the lobby," the narrative went, "the suspect suddenly grabbed the woman's boob . . ."

An outsider, unfamiliar with local dialect, might have assumed that the suspect had grabbed the woman's companion.

It definitely was not too technical for the average layman, not nearly as technical as the "piqued purloiner."

— 9 —

I Wish I Hadn't Said That

WE WERE STANDING outside the roll call room, killing the few remaining minutes before "official" shift change time. Third shift starts at 10:00 P.M., and hardly anyone wants to hit the streets early. It's a matter of principle.

"Stand by to copy a BOLO (be on the lookout)," the dispatcher said. "The Highway Patrol advises that a Knox County cruiser is running at a high rate of speed east on I–40 and has struck at least one other vehicle. They also advise the civilian who was hit is in pursuit."

All of us looked at each other and burst out laughing at the absurdity of the situation, even though it was not a laughing matter. Cops must learn to laugh at the absurd. It keeps the pressure from blowing the lid off.

"Can you imagine anyone stupid enough to let someone steal his cruiser?" Merle (we'll call him that) asked with a chuckle. "Boy, is *he* gonna have some explainin' to do."

At that moment, the dispatcher announced the tab number of the cruiser. Officers call it the "snitch number." It is plainly displayed beside the rear door, and citizens refer to it when complaining about us.

We were all still smiling, except Merle. His face had gone white. "That's *my* cruiser," he lamented.

73

The laughter erupted anew—everyone except Merle. His situation had been bad enough before he opened his mouth. It had suddenly become intolerable.

A few minutes later, the suspect (a derelict who had been staggering by the service center when he saw the unattended cruiser, left there for repairs) pulled into a market and was overtaken by the irate citizen he had hit. The citizen did what cops cannot usually get away with. He thumped the drunk driver before anyone could stop him.

It led to a new policy. No longer would officers leave the key in their cruisers for the mechanics, even though the service center was locked at night. All keys had to be left at the front desk with a tag.

For Merle, it was a situation that left him wishing he had not made the remark about "stupidity."

It happens to everyone sometimes. You open your mouth without thinking, and something ridiculous comes out. For the average citizen, it is over quickly. For a highly visible public servant, it can be devastating.

Many years ago in Knox County, a sheriff was at the scene of a murder when he vowed, "I won't sleep until this crime is solved."

Years later, with the crime still unsolved, he was still enduring the nickname "Sleepless." His political opponents loved it. Whatever good he did as sheriff was forgotten in the laughter that followed him around.

"Call the service center," the sergeant said, "and see if they have a radiator hose they can bring out here." He was calling from the lot of a nude bar.

"The service center wants to know if you have a Chevrolet or Ford," the dispatcher asked, minutes later.

"I have a Chevrolet," he answered. "Tell them I'm pretty sure there's nothing wrong except for the hose. I was checking out the Playpen, and when I walked outside, it just spurted all over my pants."

After several minutes, the dispatcher was able to regain control of her voice.

The sergeant got his radiator hose, still unaware of the implications of what he had said. He was shocked at the laughing officers waiting to greet him when he arrived at the service center. It's great when an ordinary patrolman screws up. When it's a supervisor, the humor is exquisite.

"I'll be stopping a red and white pick-up truck," the patrolman said, giving his location. "He's about to lose part of his load."

He pulled over the truck and, in keeping with the best public relations policy, told the nervous driver that he was about to have an expensive accident. Together they wrestled the heavy air conditioner to a more stable position on the truck. Afterward, the driver thanked the officer for his courtesy, waved, and drove off. It is nice to help someone once in a while.

"I helped him get his load squared away," the patrolman reported, immensely pleased at his good deed for the day.

It was only a few minutes later when the dispatcher announced a BOLO for a red and white truck. The driver had stolen three air conditioners from a grocery store.

"That's the truck I just stopped," the patrolman said to the dispatcher, without thinking.

The officer knew what was coming later.

"Officer Hayes [pseudonym] stopped a truck with stolen merchandise last night," the captain said in a serious voice at the next roll call, "but the driver was stone sober, so he turned him loose."

You can almost get under the tables at roll call—if you scrunch down hard enough.

Bushwhacking and *ambushing* are two police terms for staking out a bar and following the patrons as they leave. Strictly speaking, there is nothing wrong with the practice, as long as there are other reasons to stop the car, such as weaving or violations. The administration had made it plain (in unwritten ways) that bushwhacking and ambushing were taboo. Making a policy and enforcing it are two different things.

Most patrol officers despise drunk drivers because they see the carnage on the highway caused by them. Very often on a slow night, officers will park near a bar. You have to park *somewhere* to do your paperwork, right? If a car just happens to be leaving the bar as you just happen to be leaving the place you were parked, it is inevitable that you will notice erratic driving.

For fifteen months I worked DUI enforcement exclusively. My primary job was to apprehend drunk drivers and to administer breath tests. Now, 98 percent of all drunk drivers are caught on major thoroughfares. Almost 100 percent of all bars are on the same thoroughfares. Logic follows that an officer assigned to catch drunk drivers will patrol the areas where offenders are found.

A lawyer once tried to use this as an avenue of attack. "How many times during the course of the evening did you drive past the bar where my client was drinking?" he asked.

"Fifteen or twenty times," I replied, causing his face to light up.

"Then could you please explain to the jury *why* you continuously drove up and down that stretch of highway?"

"Sure," I answered. "I'm a DUI enforcement officer. There are few drunk drivers found in rural areas or in church parking lots."

The jury bought it. I got the conviction.

Being an intense person, I tend to do whatever I do intensely, whether writing a book, mowing the yard, or enforcing DUI laws. One night my intensity put me on record with something I wished I had not said.

Under the radio system in use at the time, we had a car-to-car channel with roughly the range of a citizens' band radio. The dispatcher could not hear us (and thus could not record) what we said to each other.

We were always pretty secure that no person of authority would be listening in the wee hours of the morning, so sometimes we were a little indiscreet. A malfunction in my radio taught me the error of my ways.

On a slow week night, I passed another cruiser on 25W. He called out to me on Channel 2 (car to car only).

"Where are you headed?" he asked.

"West," I replied after turning my switch to Channel 2. "It's slow in the north tonight. I'm going down on the pike to do some bushwhacking and ass kicking."

There was a slight pause, then the officer quickly responded. "You're goin' out on *Channel 1*!"

"Negative," I confidently replied, looking at my selector set on Channel 2. "I'm not on Channel 1."

"You *are* broadcasting on Channel 1," the dispatcher said before I could get my foot any deeper in my mouth. "Repeat. You are on Channel 1. Your selector switch is malfunctioning."

I sweated for a week. There was little chance that anyone would snitch on me. Occasionally, however, people from the hierarchy had reason to listen to a tape. There was little I could have offered by way of explanation, except maybe temporary insanity or by saying it was a joke.

Police administrations don't care much for either excuse.

He was walking hunched over against the wind, his thin jacket pulled tight around him. Thin, ragged blue jeans and a red toboggan completed the costume.

Pulling to the shoulder in front of him, I stopped and got out. I could see that he was thin, about thirty. His eyes were burned red by the wind and snow and his coffee-colored skin could not hide the ravages of the cold. His lips had taken on a bluish tinge.

"Get in the cruiser," I ordered, opening the door.

In the back seat he shook as the heat began to penetrate his clothing. "Sho' is c . . . c . . . cold!" he stuttered.

"Yes, it is. Where are you headed at this time of night and in this weather?"

"Headed for a www . . . warm place, suh."

"Don't you have any money to get in out of the cold?" I asked, turning in the seat to look at him.

"No, suh, but th' Lawd will provide. He done sent you. The angel what has been talkin' to me said help'd come."

"I hope the angel got in out of the cold."

"Yes, suh, I'm sure he did." The irony was lost on him.

"What are you doing on the road without money?"

"Well, suh. When I got outta th' hospital yestiday, I had money *and* medicine. I never sees the angel when I takes the medicine, but it please th' doctors, so I takes it. A man in a ol' car give me a ride. He sent me in fer cigarettes at this little store, then drove off and left with everythin' I had. The angel come back today."

"Baker 10," I said with a sigh. "Check with the Salvation Army. Tell them I have a male subject and he's sober."

"Ten-four," the dispatcher said.

"Is I under arrest, suh?"

"No. I'm going to find you a place to stay where it's warm. Tomorrow they'll give you breakfast and you can start early."

"Sho' do appreciate it."

We sat quietly for a few minutes. The man would turn his eyes up from time to time and nod without speaking. It appeared that the angel was still with him.

"Baker 10, the Salvation Army advises they're filled to capacity. I also called Union Rescue and Volunteers of America. They have no room, either."

"Ten-four," I replied. The extremely cold February weather had driven even the most hard-core street people inside.

If I put the man out on the street, he would die. It was as simple as that. There come times in a cop's life when cold, hard law and conscience collide. I have always tried to come down on the side of conscience whenever possible.

"You're under arrest," I said, "for disorderly conduct."

"What was I doin' wrong, offisuh?" He sounded like an injured child.

"Well, disorderly conduct covers a multitude of sins. You were disorderly by obstructing traffic and soliciting a ride on a state road." I put the car in gear. "I'm going to explain something to you on the way to jail. You'd better listen *carefully.* . . ."

I sat yawning in the courtroom as the prisoners were brought up from jail. My prisoner was dressed in the bright orange jumpsuit then furnished by the Knox County Jail. He leaned down as they brought him by.

"They sho' has good food here," he whispered. I nodded absently at him, having worked until six in the morning. Then I had gone to court at one thirty that afternoon. All my cases had been uneventful plea bargains until that moment.

As his name was called, I went before the bench, half asleep. The young man with the angelic companion quickly woke me up.

"You are charged with disorderly conduct," the judge said. "How do you plead? Are you guilty or not?"

"Well, suh," he gave the judge that same big, open smile he had given me the night before. "I never done nothin' disorderly, but I was freezin'. The nice offisuh, here, tried to find shelter for me, but there wasn't none—so he arrested me and said I had to let on like I was guilty or he'd put my young, black ass back on the street to freeze to death. So that's what I's gonna do. I pleads guilty, suh."

A thrill of terror went up my spine as the judge looked directly at me, then turned back to the prisoner.

"Do you have a family?" the judge asked.

"No, suh, just the angel that travel with me."

"Do you have *anywhere* to go?"

"No, suh. One place is good as another, I reckon. But it's mighty cold out there, suh."

"Well, sir, upon a plea of guilty, I sentence you to forty-five days at the Knox County Penal Farm. It should be warm enough to travel when you get out." The judge said the last sentence in a soft voice.

The judge let it slide. He understood conscience and law, and the conflict that sometimes arises. The subject never came up between us.

Looking back, I'm glad I did what I did. I'd do it again tomorrow. For a few seconds, though, before the judge made his decision, I wished I hadn't said that—at least not the way it came out.

— 10 —

They Call Her Calamity Jane

*I*T STARTED OUT as a simple automobile accident. Cops work lots of those. Check for injured parties, do a quick sketch, and get the street cleared as soon as possible—before some other idiot runs over the wrecked vehicle, generating *another* report.

The man reeling about, shouting incoherently, gave Officer Janie Grigsby an unpleasant premonition that this job was about to involve more that just an accident report. The driver was obviously extremely intoxicated.

The people attempting to calm the man down were family. He had wrecked his vehicle right in front of their house.

Within minutes, records told Janie a lot about the man. He had an extensive arrest record, a revoked driver's license, and was on parole—a sterling and upright citizen, all in all. She told the tall, gangly man that he was under arrest for driving under the influence and driving on a revoked license, which brought a chorus of outraged shouts from family members.

Janie called for a back-up.

A different officer might have simply told the family to

take the man inside. Out of sight, out of mind. That officer might have worked the wreck, ignoring the violation. It would have been the easiest way to handle the matter.

Janie Grigsby is not that kind of officer. She considers driving under the influence to be a serious matter and does not flinch from hard decisions.

"He took an overdose of drugs," his wiry little mother said. "You can't put him in jail."

"I can and will," Janie replied. "If he needs medical treatment, he'll get it—but he's under arrest."

As the family grumbled and cursed among themselves, Janie proceeded with the accident report. She had decided to wait on back-up before cuffing the driver. His vehicle was disabled; he was not going to drive away.

Janie turned as another vehicle started in the driveway. The mother and another woman, later identified as the man's sister, had loaded him and were backing out on to the street.

Another decision to be made.

She had identified him, and warrants could be obtained later. Her case would be weakened, though. She knew the family would all show up in court and swear to his sobriety and sterling character. It would be her word against theirs without alcohol and drug screening.

Sighing deeply, Janie sprinted to her car. Moments later, she was behind them, blue lights flashing, bumping the siren. They, of course, refused to stop. She told her back-up what was happening and told him to hurry.

It was not a high-speed pursuit. The driver simply refused to pull over. On the crooked side roads, Janie did no aggressive driving. There was no safe place to stop. As soon as they hit a main highway, however, she began to sound the siren steadily, rather than merely bumping the button, and drove right up to the bumper with all lights flashing, leaving no doubt that the driver should stop.

Finally, the car pulled to the shoulder. The back-up unit, Mike Upchurch, announced that he was almost there.

"I'm takin' him to the hospital," the mother announced. "He took an overdose of drugs."

"No, *I'm* taking him to jail," Janie replied, reaching in to get him. The man was bigger and stronger than Janie, and he began to struggle. The mother stabbed Janie's arm with a ballpoint pen, doing only minor damage but hampering her efforts.

Moments later, Mike Upchurch arrived. Together the two of them quickly jerked the suspect from the vehicle and put him in the cruiser as the mother stood screaming at them.

"You're under arrest," Janie said, walking back to the mother, "for, among other things, assault and battery and failure to yield to blue lights."

The woman, of course, did not want to go, adding resisting arrest to the other charges. As she was being cuffed, her son was apparently seized by a fit of righteous indignation at seeing his mother arrested. He began to kick at the cruiser windows.

With the help of a passing civil warrants officer, Lee Tramel, Upchurch got the man back out to calm him down, while Janie was loading the mother.

It was a fairly routine day for Janie.

Janie has blonde hair and is somewhere in her thirties. She has raised a son alone from an early bad marriage. Like a lot of cops, she did not grow up with law enforcement in mind. She drifted into it and fell in love.

We first met in 1979 as newly commissioned reserve officers at the Knox County sheriff's department. It was handgun qualification day. Most of us knew which end the bullet came out of, but little else about the Smith & Wessons we had purchased to go along with the badge.

I was sitting on a bench, holding my head in my hands, when she came along and sat down.

"What's wrong?" she asked.

"My sinuses are killing me," I answered. Reaching into

my shirt pocket, I fished out a pack of cigarettes and offered her one. She declined.

"That makes a *lot* of sense," she said, nodding her head. "If you have a sinus headache, light up a cigarette."

She walked away without saying anything else. I had just learned that she was not hesitant with her ironic humor—whether she knew you or not. It was not long until a lot of people found out that her tongue can be as sharp as a two-edged sword.

Janie did not stay long in the reserves. She hired on full time as a dispatcher. At the time, dispatchers drew patrolman's pay and worked for the sheriff's department. Now they are another division entirely.

The patrol officers for whom she dispatched quickly discovered that there was a new dispatcher who took no lip and would put them in their place over the airwaves if they got out of line. It was a rude awakening. Patrol officers generally behave as if they are the lords of creation to non-officers.

Janie decided to become a cop. The path to that goal lay through the jail, where officers generally start. She transferred to detention division and worked as an ID officer, fingerprinting and photographing prisoners until a slot came open at the police academy.

She bid on a job as a DUI enforcement officer and was among the first women officers to hold the job. Officers in that division worked straight nights and spent most of their time fighting with drunks. She did just fine, asking for no more help than her male counterparts.

Eventually she transferred to patrol, then later to Baker Shift, known as the "Killer Bees" because of their decidedly aggressive style of law enforcement.

She fit right in.

   The man was big, drunk, and belligerent. Janie had stopped him on a road in the far reaches of northern Knox County. Back-up was a long way off, and it was time for another hard choice. She carefully weighed the situation in her mind.

There were few male officers at the department who could have subdued the man without severely damaging him first. Internal Affairs and the FBI frown on pre-emptive strikes against prisoners. You have to let them make the first move.

Back-up was on the way, but how far she did not know. The man was making noises about leaving. He was much too drunk to be driving, even at three in the morning. Sometimes if you act quickly enough . . .

"You're under arrest." She snapped the cuff on his left wrist without warning. Before she could get the other arm, he exploded. They grappled on the dark country road. A handcuff becomes a dangerous weapon when attached to someone's wrist, but she held on. Drawing her weapon, of course, was out of the question. Cops can only use lethal force to save their lives or the lives of others.

Eventually, he got to his car, dragging her as he went. "Let go'a me!"

Stubbornly, she hung on to the loose cuff, even after the car started. As it picked up speed, she tightened her grip. Then he began to swerve from side to side.

Her hold broke and she was airborne, coming down hard on the back of the car as the momentum carried her over. She sat in the middle of the road, checking for damage and finding no broken bones.

The next day she signed warrants, and Baker Shift went after him. He submitted peacefully.

It was about that time that they began to call her "Calamity Jane."

Women officers and black officers have to endure abuse that most white male officers never encounter. For black officers, it is racial slurs; for female officers, it is disparaging comments about their alleged sexual preferences and femininity.

Janie is as feminine as they come. When out of the leather gear and blue suit, she's a mother and a woman. Even in uniform, she does not look masculine. Rednecks, however, enraged by having a woman slap the cuffs on them, often react with what they think will cause the most pain. One such individual found out what happens when you go into a battle of wits unarmed against a seasoned veteran.

He was a run-of-the-mill, bona fide redneck. His comments had grown louder and more abusive as he realized that no one was going to jerk him out of the car and slap his ears back, as he richly deserved.

The redneck grew louder and louder. His comments were not very imaginative. He called her a "dyke" and other such derogatory terms. She ignored his abuse and went about the inventory of his car before the wrecker got there. Another officer stood by.

In the front seat of the vehicle, Janie found a stack of Polaroid pictures. They were pornographic, showing the man engaged in various sex acts. She walked back to her cruiser, thumbing through them.

"Yeah! Look at it," he said, or something to that effect. "You'd really like to have a *real* man, wouldn't ya?"

Janie walked back and opened the cruiser, still studying the photographs carefully.

"Actually," she said, looking directly into the man's eyes, "what I was *really* thinking is that I've never seen a smaller penis on a human male."

The man collapsed, ashen-faced and speechless, his worse fears confirmed. It was what he had suspected since his first communal shower in junior high school. The horrible truth had been confirmed by a woman of authority—a woman with a badge. He had nothing else to say that evening.

It's a rough world out there on the streets at night. There is no quarter asked and none given. I saw a bumper sticker not long ago. A few years back, I might have thought it was humorous. Now, along with other thick-headed former male chauvinists, I have learned to take it seriously.

"The Best Man For the Job May Be a Woman," it says. And it may be true, especially if they call her Calamity Jane.

— 11 —

The Wicked Flee

*I*T WASN'T MUCH of a carnival—a half dozen rides, three or four booths featuring games, and a few food concessions. There were balloons, though, and the smell of cotton candy. And there was the canned music of the calliope that you always hear at carnivals and fairs.

I parked my cruiser by the side of the highway and locked it. There were a few curious stares from passers-by as I made my way toward the small midway.

There had been no complaints, but it was on my beat. I intended to let potential con men know to keep their rigged games within reason and to let the roustabouts know to keep their after hours partying under control. Even more importantly, I love carnivals.

A pretty Hispanic-looking girl was running a game in which wooden bottles were knocked over with a rubber ball. A multitude of young men were gathered there. As my uniform came into sight, she quickly buttoned her red silk blouse, which had been opened to the navel. The young men dispersed, telling me that the attraction had not been wooden bottles and stuffed dolls, but pert brown nipples slipping from the open blouse as she bent to set up bottles.

I tipped my hat to her, cavalier style, just to let her know that I had not missed the point. She flushed slightly, but nodded and smiled that she was not angry. When I was gone, the blouse would come open and the young men would come back.

Three men were standing near the back of the small midway, talking earnestly. They looked like regular denizens of the highway, dressed too well to be working men but not well enough to be outsiders come slumming from West Knoxville. I had seen them, but I did not personally know them.

The tallest of the three, a blond man of twenty or so with shoulder length hair, looked up as I approached. He was in jeans, cowboy boots, a tee-shirt with some sort of design, and a denim vest. He looked away quickly, then back, to see if I was paying attention to him.

Our eyes locked.

He whirled without comment and ran across the field. I ran after him, not bothering to waste my breath on yelling. He was a good fifteen years younger than I was, and my forte was never distance running. My stubby legs, though, were always good on the short sprint.

Until the young man ran, there was absolutely no reason for me even to speak to him. His running away, however, brought the "Terry Doctrine" into play. *Terry versus Ohio* was a long, complicated court case that ended in front of the Supreme Court. Essentially, it means that an officer is justified in investigating behavior known to him to be suspicious, based on past experience.

He had about a twenty-foot lead, but I was closing. His youth was somewhat offset by running in high-heeled cowboy boots. As we hit the road behind the carnival lot, he pulled something from his belt and tossed it aside. It landed with a heavy metallic thud and skittered on the pavement. I had no doubt that it was a small pistol.

Plastic baggies began to hit the ground behind him as he jerked them from his pockets as he ran into a field across the road. The moonlight glistened on the packets as he dropped them along the way, trying to rid himself of evidence.

My burst of energy was almost depleted when he stepped in a hole and fell forward on his face with a grunt. Gasping for breath, I grabbed his wrist and pulled it behind him. He was cuffed before he had enough wind to struggle.

"What have we here?" I asked, pulling the remaining rolled up plastic bag from his front pocket where it protruded. "This looks suspiciously like marijuana. You wouldn't be engaging in a little free enterprise tonight, would you?"

"I was set up, wasn't I?" His voice was breaking, on the verge of crying.

"And that pistol you threw down back there. Do you have a permit?" I was enjoying myself thoroughly.

"I just wanna know, who set me up?" he asked.

"Baker 13," I ignored his question as I called dispatch, "I need a car to meet me . . ."

By the time help arrived, I had found nine plastic bags of marijuana and had recovered the pistol. It was a cheap .25 caliber automatic, but it was just as good as the best pistol ever manufactured for making a charge of carrying a weapon during the commission of a felony stick—to wit, possession of a schedule drug for the purpose of resale. Not even the fact that I knew both charges would later be reduced to misdemeanors dampened my spirits. It was a good bust.

It was what cops call a freebie or a gimme. All I had to do was be there.

"Who set me up is what I wanna know." the man asked again. "You *knew* I was carryin' before you got there. You were lookin' for me, right?"

"Let's put it this way. You'd better check your list of close friends. One of them may not be as friendly as you think."

I knew this tactic—sowing discord in the enemy camp—would hamper his dealings for a long time as he tried to figure out who had snitched him out. I also knew he

wouldn't believe that he had brought about his own down-
fall. Criminals take no responsibility for their own short-
comings.

A verse of scripture came to mind. I was tempted to
quote it for him, but decided against it. He was probably
not familiar with Proverbs, anyway, where it says in chapter
28, verse 1: "The wicked flee when no man pursueth: but
the righteous are bold as a lion."

The shaggy man in denim jeans and an old fa-
tigue shirt glanced nervously at Mike Upchurch and my
brother Larry as they got out of the cruiser. The two officers were riding together because Larry's cruiser had broken down early in the shift. They had pulled in just behind
the man, who was driving an old Plymouth.

"That's ol' John Gooch [a pseudonym]," Upchurch
drawled, reaching for his radio. "I just got him convicted of
drunk drivin' last week. I wonder if the state has got
around to revoking his license yet?"

Conviction for driving under the influence carries a one-
year minimum license revocation in Tennessee. Unfortunately, it takes a few weeks for the state to get around to
putting the revoked license number into the computer. Until that happens the license is not "officially" revoked.

As Upchurch talked to records, a girl of twelve or thirteen got out of the old Plymouth and followed the man into
the little market. In a few moments, records informed Upchurch that the license was still valid.

"That girl looks a little young to be out with him," Larry
said as they entered the market.

"That's his daughter," Upchurch said. "He's got several
kids. One night me and David went to his house on a domestic. John's wife had just divorced him. He went into the
house with a little bottle of water and drank it in front of his
ex-wife and kids. He told 'em it was poison, then ran off in
the woods.

"By the time we got there, all the kids were hysterical

because they thought he was out in the woods dyin'. We called in a dog and hunted on foot for an hour. It was July, and we nearly died of heatstroke in the body armor. He'd doubled back to the road and got a ride home.

"I found out later that he bragged about how scared his kids were and how ignorant we were to be out in that heat lookin' for him.

"He's a real dirt-bag. All I can say is that it's too bad his license ain't revoked yet. I'd be glad to lock him up again."

As they ordered their coffee, the clerk bagged up two hamburgers and two orders of french fries for Gooch. As Gooch and his daughter left, he continued to glance nervously at the two officers.

Meanwhile I was northbound, approaching the little market where Larry and Mike were having their coffee. I was unaware of the little drama that was transpiring.

As I topped the hill, the old battered Plymouth pulled from the lot, spinning its wheels—probably by accident. As the vehicle crossed the highway, northbound in front of me, Gooch accelerated quickly. I also saw that he had only one taillight.

Kicking in the four-barreled carburetor, I closed the gap and hit the blue lights. He did not slow down. I heard the engine of his vehicle strain harder.

"Baker 13, I'm in pursuit. Advise Anderson County that I'm crossing the line, northbound on 25W." I gave a description of the vehicle.

As we dropped off the ridge into Anderson County, I was already shaking with fear and rage. There is nothing I hat worse than a high-speed pursuit. Unfortunately, if officers failed to pursue fleeing vehicles, *everyone* would soon refuse to stop.

"Baker 16 to Baker 13," Upchurch said over the air, "the subject in that car is John Gooch. He probably thinks you're after him for a revoked license. I'm comin' to assist you."

"Ten-four," I replied, becoming even angrier. I did not

have to ask what kind of low-life risks death on the highway to avoid a traffic charge. I was well familiar with Gooch. He was a childish, irresponsible drunk who thought of nobody but himself.

His speed, which had reached ninety-five miles per hour, began to drop off as we approached an intersection. I "feather-tapped" my brakes, preparing for a turn. As he made the abrupt left hand swing, I gained on him, outdriving him through the controlled slide.

Just a few feet from his bumper, I yelled over my public address system. "Pull it over, Gooch, before somebody gets hurt."

He ignored me but could not put any distance between us. I tried to drive around him as he made another right hand turn, but he blocked me. Moments later, he swung the old car into a housing project.

There were no people out at that hour. The sound of the siren bounced back with a ghostly sound from the brick walls, and the blue lights contributed an eerie glow as we drove between buildings, over sidewalks, and up and down embankments.

I had run him to ground. He lived somewhere in the complex. I prepared to bail out as he hit his brakes. I was determined that he would not escape on foot.

As he rolled to a halt, the interior light of his car came on, startling me. He had opened the passenger door. Under the dim glow of the interior light, I saw him shove someone out of the car. I had been unaware until then that he had a passenger.

He accelerated away, leaving me to brake hard to keep from running over the figure in front of me. It was a female in a white blouse. She immediately jumped up and ran like a deer. I had very nearly hit her.

Seeing that she was not injured, I squalled away in pursuit again. A couple hundred yards ahead, however, the old Plymouth sat, driver's side door open, still running and with the interior lights on.

He had gotten away. I could not bang on doors and demand entrance. The Constitution is very specific about that. I had no idea which apartment he had entered.

Within minutes, Larry and Mike and several Anderson County deputies had arrived.

"What did you have him on?" one of the Anderson deputies asked.

"Until he started running, a simple citation for a bad taillight. Now I'll need warrants for reckless driving, fleeing to avoid arrest, and child abuse. I'm sure that was a child he pushed out in front of my cruiser."

"She *is* a child," Upchurch said, "about twelve years old. We can verify that she was in the car and that this *is* the car. Anybody want a hamburger and fries? There's two orders here—still hot."

"This guy must be one dumb son-of-a-bitch," the Anderson County deputy said.

"Yeah," I replied, calling for a wrecker. I put a hold on the car, pending criminal charges. I knew he would not attempt to pick it up. He was aware that I would be waiting for him with warrants. He would just go buy another old junker, and it would probably have burned-out taillights, too.

Wicked, according to my dictionary, is an adjective, meaning "morally bad, evil." It is not a popular word these days. Words like *maladjusted* or *disturbed* are tossed around as if they mean the same thing.

The definitions are not even close. Tossing a child—any child, much less one's own flesh and blood—into the path of a moving vehicle ranks right up there with the most debased of crimes—sins, if you wish. It shows a total self-absorption, to the exclusion of all that is selfless and good in human nature.

John Gooch's behavior, and that of the dope dealer, bears out what observers of human nature have always known. No one has yet said it anymore succinctly than the anonymous writer of Proverbs 28:1: "The wicked flee when no man pursueth. . . ."

—12—

To Enter Unarmed a Battle of Wits

I LISTENED CLOSELY as the "alert" sound buzzed over my radio. It is an unpleasant sound, like the humming of a giant insect. It also buzzes when the power runs down. It is not a sound to be ignored.

"North units—a 10–52 [armed robbery] just occurred at I–75 and . . ." My pulse quickened as she gave the location. I was *close*. "The suspect is a black male. He was last seen northbound on . . ."

I jammed my foot on the gas pedal, listening to the engine strain. Movie and television cops drive up on armed robberies all the time. In real life, it seldom happens.

Within minutes I was in the vicinity—making a decision. The little market that had just been robbed is at the junction of I–75 and a secondary road. To be exact, another road runs parallel between it and the interstate ramp.

An eight-foot chain-link fence separates the small road and the interstate ramp. Given the suspect's direction of travel, he either had to go up the little road or cross the chain-link fence. As I tried to make up my mind, Homicide Detective Mike Lett cut in. "During the last robbery there, a car waited up on the interstate to pick up the suspect."

That he had a confederate or a car waiting to pick him up was almost a certainty. Despite my speed, another patrol unit radioed that he had passed the intersection and would cover the next exit.

I slowed to a crawl as I went by the interstate ramp, scanning the underbrush at the side of the road. In my rearview mirror I saw movement—not clearly, but clearly enough to recognize a running figure.

I continued on as if I had seen nothing. A half mile or so up the road, I killed my lights and shot across the median, falling in with the southbound traffic.

Moments later, I passed the suspect. He was a black male, shirtless. He was running like an antelope, looking over his left shoulder at the passing traffic. He did not see my cruiser as I passed in the outside lane.

"Send me a back-up," I said. "I have a black male suspect running southbound at the south exit ramp."

Arriving at the exit ramp, I parked my car on the median, drew my weapon and walked on the shoulder to meet him. I could hear him gasping for air, as he ran toward me in long, loping strides, still looking back over his shoulder. Apparently he was watching for his confederate who had probably driven off when the first police car went by.

"Police officer! Stop right there!" I yelled, sighting down the barrel of my Smith & Wesson revolver as he got within fifteen feet of me.

"Don't shoot!" he screamed, skidding to a halt on the asphalt shoulder. "Don't kill me!"

"Drop to your knees! Keep your hands out where I can see them!"

"I'll do it. Just *please* don't shoot!"

"Cross your ankles. Lace your fingers together on the back of your head."

A patrol unit was coming northbound toward me on the south exit ramp, so I waited for it to arrive before I attempted to search or cuff. Janie Grigsby got out of the cruiser, drawing her weapon. As I covered him, she snapped on the cuffs and raised him up.

"Why you arrestin' me?" he asked, still out of breath.

"Why are you running down the interstate in the middle of the night?"

"My buddy done broke down back up the road. I was goin' for help." He was young and muscular, drenched in sweat.

"Take him back to the store and see if the clerk can ID him," I told Janie.

Despite the far-fetched nature of his story, I called the unit north of us and told the officer there to check for vehicles broken down beside the road. There were none.

The clerk made a positive identification. Using the point where he had crossed the road behind me as a reference, Sergeant Larry Davis and other Baker Shift officers soon located the money bag, the pistol, and the shirt he had been wearing.

As we did the paperwork that night, I marveled at the criminal mind.

In order to escape, all the man had to do was sit still. We did not have enough help to search the entire length of the interstate. If he had simply sat somewhere in the miles of underbrush, we would have assumed his confederate had picked him up. Instead, he ran along the shoulder of an interstate highway in full view of traffic, in the middle of the night, as if it were the normal thing to do.

His capture led to the solution of several armed robberies in two counties.

I followed closely as the old yellow Ford station wagon almost came to a stop. He had overtaken me on 25W, then had slowed to keep from passing me. This had led to my slowing down so that I could get behind him. I wanted to know what it was he didn't want me to see.

A sure way to attract a cop's attention is to try to avoid him. In this case, the problem was a burned out taillight, which probably would not have interested me at all on a busy Friday night. Closer attention, however, revealed that the tag was also expired.

Even at that, I might have ignored minor violations. There are too many drunks and thieves on 25W during weekends. However, his steering was distinctly wavering across the shoulder line. I could see him watching me in his rearview mirror.

As I reached for the blue lights switch, he whipped into a small market by the road. I followed and turned on the blue lights, so there would be no doubt in his mind what I wanted. We stepped from the vehicles at the same time. His eyes darted right and left. I could see rabbit fever.

"Don't run from me," I said. "If you do, it'll make things worse."

He bolted. I was hot on his heels. Running behind the little store, he looked over his shoulder and jumped. I heard him splash down in the waist-high water of the creek. As I approached the embankment, he was wading away.

"You better come back," I yelled. "There's nowhere for you to go."

I went back to my car and got my coat and clipboard, almost feeling sorry for him. It was mid-February, and the temperature was less that twenty degrees Fahrenheit.

As I inventoried his car, I found the reasons he had fled: a nearly empty bottle of cherry-flavored vodka and a plastic bag with several marijuana cigarettes. In the glove compartment was a cheap .22 caliber pistol, a bill of sale for the old car with his current address, and a driver's license, which records notified me had been revoked for drunk driving. The expired tag did not belong on the old Ford.

After the wrecker came and towed the vehicle, I pulled in behind an abandoned store building about three hundred yards up the road. There were only two places where a man who was soaking wet in freezing weather could go at that time of night, and I could see both from my vantage point.

He had two choices: a phone at the little store from

which he had run and a bar just up the highway. The bar appeared to be closing as I watched. The man could, of course, have walked home, but I did not think so, not while soaking wet in twenty-degree weather over a distance of ten miles or so to the address on his bill of sale.

I was finishing a cup of coffee from my thermos when he emerged from the field behind the bar and rattled the front door, which was locked. Unable to gain entrance, he walked over to a car in which several people were sitting.

Calling for back-up, I shot across the highway. He tried to run again but was hampered by frozen trousers. As I was putting him in my cruiser, another officer pulled in and checked the people in the car. They were all exceedingly drunk and soon were on their way to jail for the weekend.

"What's this all abbbb . . . out?" His teeth chattered.

"It's about drunk driving, possession of marijuana, driving on a revoked driver's license, improper car registration, carrying a weapon, and fleeing to avoid arrest. Oh, yeah, and since I caught you away from the scene, I'm also charging you with public drunkenness."

"You'll nnn . . . ever mmm . . . ake it sttt . . . ick. Ittt . . . s my word againnnn . . . st yyyy . . . ours!"

"My word's always been good enough before. But feel free to try and make the judge believe anything you want. It'll be the second time in three days that you went to a battle of wits unarmed."

Any officer can tell stories of criminal types who engineer their own downfalls. For sheer lack of reasoning, however, the most impressive (or least impressive) display of witless behavior occurred when Mike Upchurch and I went to serve an assault warrant one evening.

The offender was a petty criminal. Generally, he was picked up for public drunkenness or drunk driving. A few days earlier, however, in a drunken fit he had assaulted someone who had in turn signed a warrant. As usual, he was hiding out.

Unfortunately, he was hiding on Mike Upchurch's old beat, where Mike has kept extensive contacts. Someone had called Mike and snitched on him. So, on a slow evening, Upchurch called me and a couple of patrol units to pick up the offender.

"As soon as we roll up the driveway," Upchurch told the patrolmen, "cover the sides and the front. Hunter will go to the back door with me. That's where they go in and out. This house belongs to his grandmother. His mother lives next door. If he gets out, someone will hide him."

Moments later we wheeled in. Patrol officers in place, Upchurch and I walked to the back of the house. Beside the back door was a wooden deck. Behind the sliding glass doors sat our suspect. He was kicked back in an easy chair, drinking a beer.

"Come on out, Teddy. We have a warrant, and the house is surrounded," Upchurch said loudly.

The suspect stood and looked at us.

"Let's go," I said. "Walk around and open the door. You can't get away."

The lanky, blond suspect, a man in his mid-twenties, walked from the room, presumably to let us in.

"Keep your eye on those sliding glass doors," Upchurch warned. "He may try to dart out there."

We waited for about five minutes, then began to pound on the back door. There was no answer.

"I'll get something to open it with," I said, walking back to my cruiser. I found a tire tool and was about to close the trunk when a middle-aged woman walked across the field from next door.

"Have you cops found what you want?" she demanded. "There are enough of you."

"We wouldn't need so many if your sons didn't always run. How many times have we been here through the years?"

"My mother-in-law's in there. She's a sick woman. She shouldn't be disturbed."

"If Teddy will come out like we asked, nobody has to be disturbed."

"Teddy's gone to South Carolina," she said. The woman was dumpy and unkempt, even though she had once been attractive. We had been arresting all her sons for years.

"We just saw him. Do you have a key, or shall I use mine?" I held up the tire tool. "Yours would be cheaper."

With a sigh, she reached into her pocket and came out with a key ring. Two minutes later we were walking through the small, cramped house. Teddy was not hiding in the main rooms. That left the bedroom where his invalid grandmother lived.

"I hate to do this," I told Mike, "but I guess we have no choice." We stopped at the door.

"Ma'am," Upchurch drawled, "we're police officers comin' in to get Teddy. Don't be frightened."

"He's not here," she said with a tongue thickened by at least one stroke.

We walked to the back of the room and pulled aside the curtain covering the closet. Teddy sat there, knees pulled up to his chin as if we would never see him if he maintained a low profile.

"What's this all about?" he asked as we pulled him to his feet.

"Well, you wouldn't come to the door," Upchurch said.

"I didn't know you wanted me."

"Then why were you hiding? Did you think we'd just go away if you didn't come to the door?" I asked.

"I don't know what you're talking about. I was just sittin' here in my granny's closet mindin' my own business. Have you got a search warrant?"

"Let's get out of this room. You're upsettin' your grandmother," Upchurch said.

When he did not move, we caught him by the arms and propelled him down the hallway, where we put him against the wall.

"Momma, momma," he yelled, "they're abusin' me."

His mother stood at the back door, saying nothing as we took her baby boy out to the cruiser.

"Momma," he yelled over his shoulder, "go get my cigarettes and bring them to me."

"Forget it," I told her. "We've wasted all the time we're gonna waste here. Load him and get gone," I told the patrol officer.

"You can wait until I hunt his cigarettes," the woman snapped.

"No, we can't. Somebody should have been saying no to his whining years ago."

The cruiser pulled away with Teddy yelling to his momma from the back. The rest of us pulled away in a few moments.

Later, over coffee Upchurch chuckled and shook his head. "That ole Teddy is a sharp one. If you don't want to go to jail, just don't open the door and hide in the closet. The cops will think they were *imaginin'* that they saw you walking around inside."

"Just another man in a battle of wits—totally unarmed," I said.

"Yeah," Upchurch laughed again, stirring cream into his coffee, "but *some* of them are in a class all by themselves."

— 13 —

The Claiborne Gang and the House-brand Beer

"TEN-85 [DISTURBANCE in progress] at the shopping center," the dispatcher intoned. "Complainant says the suspects are throwing beer cans from under the bridge. Complainant says his vehicle was struck by several cans."

It was a new beat for me, and I was unfamiliar with a group that beat officers called the Claiborne Gang (not their real name). Two of them were brothers, the rest just part of the gang.

Two patrol units wheeled into the shopping center just ahead of me and shot across the pavement toward a small bridge over a creek where the parking lot exited to the highway. Four or five men suddenly ran in all different directions as the units approached them. One was running in my direction, so I killed my lights, got out of the cruiser, and waited.

A moment later, he ran into my arms, still looking over his shoulder. He was a small, muscular man, exceedingly drunk and about twenty-five years of age. He struggled briefly as I cuffed him.

"What's this all about?" he yelled. "I ain't done nothin' wrong."

As I pulled up to the bridge, I saw that the other two officers had three more subjects in their cars. The officers were looking off the bridge. Looking down, I saw a home-made plastic tent, a campfire, and dozens of beer cans.

"What's happening?" I asked.

"What we have here is the campsite of the notorious Claiborne Gang, also known as the "Trolls" because they live under bridges during the summer. During the cold months all of them live with their families."

"What do they do?" I asked.

"They get drunk and steal—anything that isn't nailed down. It doesn't even matter if they can sell it or not. If they can get their hands on it, they take it."

"Yeah," the other officer said. "One year I found thirteen Christmas trees stuffed under this bridge. They kept stealing them but never sold any."

"Are they mentally retarded?" I asked.

"Nope," one officer answered. "They're just a bunch of lazy drunks. None of them has ever had a full-time job. Sometimes they cut grass in the summer, but usually not for long. They end up stealing from the people they're working for. All they want is enough money to get drunk."

I watched, fascinated, as my fellow officers hunted around until they had found several big rocks, then dropped them on the homemade plastic tent until it was destroyed.

Later, I learned to do the same thing. It was like a pre-emptive strike on a hornets' nest. It was easier to discourage them in advance than to have them come back as soon as they were out of jail.

"The Claiborne Gang has really been a pain to-night," I told the officer running the beat next to mine.

"I know," he yawned. "I'm glad they're on your beat instead of mine tonight."

The north beat and the northeast beat were divided by a major highway. The Claiborne Gang moved from one side of the highway to another. There were two bridges, both running over the same small creek at different locations. The gang had a third place along the same creek, where there was no bridge. They used the third location when we put too much heat on the bridge camping areas. They were harder to reach at that location because officers had to walk in on foot for several hundred yards.

On that particular night, they were not under the bridge but at their third location. Access to the third area was off a road running across the major highway. The two Claibornes and their cronies were rip-roaring drunk. They were playing a large (probably stolen) portable stereo as loudly as they could, disturbing people a quarter of a mile away.

Every time I showed up, the gang scattered into the surrounding woods and fields. It was a busy night, replete with minor accidents, shopliftings, and domestic disputes. There had been no time for extended foot pursuits on misdemeanors. They knew this as well as I did.

"My only hope is that they'll run out of beer," I said.

"Yeah," the other officer replied, "then they'll send one of their cronies up to the supermarket to steal another case."

That was exactly what happened less than an hour later.

"Baker 13, 10–55 [larceny] of a case of beer, the supermarket on . . ."

I was close, speeding toward the location and knowing exactly where the thief would run with the beer. He would have to cross the back parking lot of the supermarket, wait for a break in traffic, then dash across to the woods.

Within a couple of minutes, I was waiting on foot, my cruiser parked at a small convenience store across the street. The thief did not disappoint me.

It was not one of the Claibornes, although he was a member of the gang. A burly man of average height, he always needed a shave. Before falling in with the Claibornes, he had once worked odd jobs. Like them, however, he had never had what you would call a full-time occupation—except for being publicly drunk and a thief.

He appeared from the back lot of the supermarket and looked up and down the road. Not seeing me standing by a telephone pole in the dark, he started across, running as fast as is possible carrying an armload of canned beer. He came to a halt as I stepped into his path.

"Don't even think about it," I told him. "If you run, I'm going to be *really* upset."

Sighing deeply, his shoulders slumped, he went with me to my cruiser. As I was cuffing him, the officer from the adjoining beat drove in and got out. He looked at the case of beer by my car.

"You stole the *house-brand beer?*" my fellow officer asked. "Why didn't you steal premium beer? The penalty's all the same."

"I dunno. Habit I guess," my prisoner answered as he sat in the back of my cruiser.

"And you didn't even get to drink any of it," the officer said, pushing back his hat.

"I did so," my prisoner snapped, "I opened a beer and drunk it in the store. That was when the clerk hollered, and I grabbed this case and run away."

"What brand did you drink?" the officer asked, apparently fascinated.

"Same kind I got here." This time he dropped his head, apparently ashamed of his inadequacy as a thief.

"You don't drink beer do you, Hunter?"

"No."

"Well, this stuff would gag a maggot. I just can't believe anybody would *voluntarily* drink it. Of course," he shrugged his shoulders, "I don't know anybody else who lives under a bridge either."

"Look," I nodded toward the woods. "Joe Claiborne is

watching us." He stood about fifty yards from the road, giving himself plenty of lead if I tried to chase him.

"Hey, Joe," my fellow officer yelled. "Come up here and get this beer. There's no use letting it go to waste. Your buddy here is going to jail."

"Naw, you'll just grab me if I come up there," Claiborne yelled. He was wearing a dirty T-shirt and filthy cut-off blue jeans. The facilities are not too good when you are camped by a stream.

"Heck, no. We wouldn't do that, Joe. Look, the beer's still cold." The officer held up a six pack, which was beaded with sweat. "If you don't get it, it just goes to waste."

"He's not that stupid," I said quietly.

"Wait and see," the officer said from the side of his mouth. "The party is over, anyway, without the beer. Jail means nothing to the Claibornes. They've both been there dozens of times. If he thinks there's the slightest chance he can get the beer, he'll come up here."

"Will you give me your word as a . . ." he struggled for unfamiliar words . . . "*gentleman* not to arrest me?" Joe Claiborne yelled.

"You got it," my brother officer said.

He came out of the woods and across the parking lot, barefoot, with mud up to his knees. Even from a distance it was obvious that he was extremely drunk.

As he padded across the asphalt, I took out my extra cuffs and caught him by the arm.

"You *promised* . . ."

"Naw, Joe," the other officer said. "*I* promised, not this officer. Besides, I ain't a gentleman, anyway."

"Thanks," I said. "Maybe the rest of them will go away."

"Yeah, they'll probably go back over to my side under one of the bridges, but they'll be quiet for a while, I guess."

"I don't see how *anybody* can drink that house-brand beer," he said again before driving off.

The store manager refused to prosecute for larceny, so I booked both my prisoners for being publicly drunk.

When I logged in the beer as evidence, the property clerk made snickering remarks about its quality. He said I'd never convince a jury that anyone actually stole it.

By the time I left patrol, a third Claiborne brother had joined the gang and followed in his brothers' footsteps. One of the gang members was killed in a car wreck and another got religion and went to work. The two were soon replaced by new recruits.

On a slow night, officers who run the north and northeast beats always go by and tear down the homemade plastic tents. If the gang doesn't disperse in time, they will be arrested. They are always drunk, always trespassing somewhere.

The Claibornes have one sister, the baby of the family. Recently, she married a young man from the community. A short while after the marriage, he was arrested for drunk driving. The three Claibornes were with him, as were two members of the gang.

A brother-in-law with a car has been a distinct boon to the Claiborne gang. They were all on their way to the lake to get drunk, which is a lot classier than getting drunk by a creek.

The trunk was full of house-brand beer from the big supermarket. When asked if they had stolen it, the brother-in-law indignantly told the officer that he was not a thief. Further, he said, he used to drink premium beer until his brothers-in-law showed him the folly of wasting money. All beer in Tennessee has the same amount of alcohol, after all.

A lucky man, that new brother-in-law, to have a ready-made family whose members do not squander money on frivolous things.

─14─

The Old Man at the End of the Lane

I RAN UP ON the old man by accident one lazy morning. First shift at the Knox County Sheriff's Department runs from 6:00 A.M. until 2:00 P.M. Mornings are busy times for detectives as night burglaries are discovered, but slow for patrolmen, aside from a few traffic accidents.

Morning shifts were hateful times for me. My inner clock is just getting wound up at midnight, and I don't slow down until about three in the morning. Getting up at five o'clock was never pleasant. It would take me until about nine to drink enough coffee to feel human again. Fortunately, we rotated every seven days.

I always took my days off on morning shift. That way I could keep the early rising days down to five every month. The five almost did me in.

It was about eleven when I turned up an unfamiliar lane. A good patrolman knows his beat well, but no matter how you try there will still be places you haven't seen.

Crunching over the gravel, it became obvious that the little lane was a driveway, left over when the side of the ridge was carved away to make room for a trailer park. A rundown house came into sight. The doors and windows stood open, protected by old-fashioned screens. There was no sign of air conditioning.

I was seized by a feeling of having been there before without knowing why. I had grown up across the valley, but no distinct memory of the place came to me. As an old man slowly, but deliberately, hobbled in my direction, I realized that he, too, looked familiar.

Stooped, walking with the aid of a cane, his eyes were nonetheless alert. I took him to be in his seventies, at least.

"Somethin' the matter, officer?"

"No, sir. Just killing a little time by looking over my beat," I replied.

"Git out and set a spell then. I was just gittin' ready to move some scrap down to chop for kindlin'. Wasn't havin' much luck, though. There's a big tree done fell acrost my scrap wood."

I got out reluctantly. Since I had already told him I was killing time, there seemed little excuse I could offer for not stopping.

"Let me git you a dope and a cheer," the old man said as I got out of my cruiser. He was headed for the door before I could decline. *Dope* is an old East Tennessee word for any soft drink. I hadn't heard it in years and have no idea about its origin.

Not far from the house was a shed. It had the looks of a place that had once been used by a man who labored with his hands, but it had since fallen into disuse. An old crosscut saw hung on the wall, as did a briar scythe and several hand sickles.

He emerged in a moment, dragging a worn kitchen chair and carrying a soft drink can. It was the kind of cola you buy in quantity at supermarkets, sold under the store brand by the case.

"I'd invite you in, but the house is a mess. My wife died three years ago. She always tended the inside, and I tended to things outside. Besides, the heat'll kill you this time of day inside."

"I shouldn't stay long," I told him, taking a sip of the horrible store-brand cola. "I've got a pretty big beat to cover."

"You grow up around here?"

"Yes, sir. Right across the valley. We moved away when I was sixteen."

"Things has changed a lot. Mine was the only house for a mile at one time. I raised two boys here." I waited, but he did not name them. "Both of 'em is successful now. Real successful."

As we made small talk, I wondered why his boys had not furnished him with an air conditioner to ease his old age. I began to plot how I could talk someone into donating one, or where I might find a used one at a good price.

"Well, I need to be moving along. Thanks for the drink."

"You come and see me, hear? I don't git much company."

As I backed up, I saw him standing before the pile of scrap lumber, across which the tree had fallen.

As I got out of my beat-up Ford, the old man hobbled from the house. I smelled the odor of grease wafting from inside. He stood peering uneasily at me as I approached in jeans and T-shirt.

"Officer Hunter," I said, "I was here this morning." I opened the trunk and got out a chainsaw I had borrowed from a cop who lived in the neighborhood.

"Did you forgit somethin'?"

"No, I was helping a friend with some winter firewood," I lied. "I thought I'd just drop by and get that old tree out of your way. Just go ahead and fix your supper. I won't be long."

Even with my lack of expertise with things mechanical, the tree did not take long. I found an ax and a wedge and reduced it to manageable pieces, then carried it down to the house and deposited it beside the door.

"Would you join me?" the old man asked from inside. "I've fried up some okra and pork chops."

"No, thanks. Go ahead and eat. I'm going to carry down some of that kindling while I'm here."

As I carried the last armload down, the old man dragged out the chair again and another canned cola of the same brand as before. I sat down, telling him I would have to leave shortly.

"Did you know my boy, Danny? He's purty near your age."

Suddenly everything dropped into place. I knew why everything was so familiar.

Danny—a skinny kid, a year younger than I—had front teeth so deformed that it probably took everything he had to face the world each day. His front teeth protruded so badly that his mouth never closed fully, and he looked like a caricature of the buck-toothed farm boy. He was one of those children who endure torment from their peers until they either develop character or break altogether.

Danny had developed character, had become an expert in many fields, and a scholar. It was not surprising to me that Danny had become a successful man, or so his father said.

We had been friends, but he never invited me home and always had a reason why I could not visit him. One Saturday morning I went unannounced to his house.

The driveway was very long in those days, meandering up the side of the hill and lined with tall trees. It was the only house for a mile in either direction. A dog yapped as I walked into the clearing. Things were neat then, not run-down and old.

The man looked up from the back of a pick-up truck on which he was loading tools as I approached. His glare was angry.

"What can I do for you?" he asked gruffly.

"I'm a friend of Danny's. I was going to see if he wanted to go hiking with me today."

"Danny helps me on Saturdays. He's inside gittin' ready.

He ain't got time for play. We got a livin' to earn." The man turned his back on me.

Stunned, I turned and walked away. I had never been addressed in such a manner by the father of a friend. Before I got to the end of the driveway, I heard the truck coming and hid in the weeds beside the road. Danny was in the passenger seat. His father was talking angrily to him— about what, I do not know. Perhaps he was discussing frivolous, unannounced visitors.

They didn't see me, and I never mentioned the visit to Danny. Nor did he bring it up, if he ever knew about it.

That afternoon, drinking the sickening cola, it was as if twenty-five years had melted away. The memory washed over me, transporting me to adolescence.

"Did you know Danny?"

The old man was leaning forward, looking at me. Apparently he had been waiting for an answer.

"Yes, sir. I remember Danny. If you'll excuse me, I'm running a little late."

"What do I owe you for your work?" He reached for his wallet.

"Not a thing, sir. I'm sure you'll be able to do me a favor some day."

"I appreciate it," he said as I drove away.

I stayed away from the old man after that, castigating myself for irrational feelings. People change. The decrepit old man sitting alone was not the same person I had met that Saturday morning twenty-five years ago.

Still, I could not bring myself to go back. I kept thinking of Danny and the long ago days when he endured what no child should endure.

It was about three weeks later when I was dispatched to the house.

The old kitchen chair was already outside when I arrived. He was waiting at the door, and when I pulled up he went in and returned with one of those accursed, sickly sweet colas.

He had called on the pretext of getting advice about what he could do to keep children from trespassing on his property. It was obvious, though, that he merely wanted to talk. After I had answered his questions about trespassers, he opened another line of conversation.

"Did you know my younger son?"

"No, sir. He was still in grammar school when I left here."

"He's done well for hisself, but not as well as Danny. Danny's got his own business now."

Then, out of the blue the old man dredged up the past, startling me with his perception.

"Danny had buckteeth, you know?" He glanced at me, but I did not speak. "He's had 'em fixed now, and he's as good lookin' a man as you'd ever wanna know.

"Some people thought I didn't care about how he looked—but I *did* care. I took him to one of them orthodontist fellows one time when he was little.

"The man said it'd cost five hundred dollars, and he couldn't guarantee that the teeth would straighten out. Five hundred dollars was a lot of money then. I told him that if I built him a bathroom I'd guarantee it to work or he didn't have to pay, but he wouldn't budge.

"I coulda been wrong, I guess . . . but five hundred dollars was a *lot* of money. I guess you kin understand that?"

"Yes, sir, it was a lot of money." I sipped the horrible cola, not looking at him.

"I know I pushed them boys hard. I never give either of 'em much time to play. But *life* is hard. I reckon I done somethin' right. They're both successful. I coulda been wrong, though, about not havin' them teeth of Danny's straightened when he was little . . ."

"Well, I need to be on my way." I stood.

"I'd appreciate it if you'd stop by from time to time. It

gits kinda lonesome. I never took much time for friends when I was younger, and my boys are real busy."

"I'll do that, sir."

And I did, as long as I worked that beat. My ill feelings for the old man had been replaced by pity.

He never again brought up the subject of Danny's teeth. We kept our conversations generic and simple.

"What you sow, you will reap," my father always said, paraphrasing the Bible.

It's true.

Dear God, I pray whenever I think about the lonely old man, *help me to remember that my wealth does not lie in what I can hoard away, but in those I love and those who love me. Amen.*

—15—

The Children's Teeth Are Set on Edge

"**W**HAT'S THAT, DAD?"

"What are you talking about, son?" Paris, then four, was passing the time with me as I prepared to go out on night shift, mimicking my actions. A blond child with eyes somewhere between blue and brown, he stood looking puzzled. Pinned to his shirt was a toy deputy's badge; around his waist was a plastic holster and pistol.

"The thing you just put on, the thing with the straps."

"It's my body armor, Paris. I *always* wear body armor." Then it dawned on me. I had new body armor in a blue carrier. My old armor had been encased in white.

"What's body armor?"

"You know what armor is. Knights wore armor." I slipped my shirt on and tucked it in.

"Their armor was shiny and made of metal," he said."You couldn't cut it with a sword. What's yours for?"

"We call this a bullet-proof vest, son." I tapped it with my knuckles. "It's supposed to stop bullets."

"Stop bullets?"

"Right." I pinned on my badge and reached for my gun-belt.

Suddenly, I saw that he was staring at me, eyes wide and bright. A realization had come upon him. He knew for the first time that television shows are not all fantasy. He had made the connection between the hundreds of police and western shows he had seen and the real universe.

Guns fire bullets. Bullets are real. Policemen wear bullet-proof vests because someone may shoot them—for real.

Without speaking, he ran from the room. I walked down the hall to his bedroom and found him sitting on the edge of his bed, staring straight ahead. I sat down and put my arm around him.

"What's wrong, Hoss?" Only I am allowed to use that nickname. Once in a store, a clerk overheard me talking to him and called him "Hoss" as we were leaving.

"Only my *dad* calls me that," he said. Once he called me "Daddy," but somewhere along the line, he decided that "Dad" sounded more mature.

"I don't want someone to shoot you or Uncle Larry or Bobby or the Upchurch." He looked up with bright, tear-rimmed eyes, his lower lip trembling. He has always called Mike Upchurch, "the Upchurch." We never figured out why.

"Son," I was trying to choose my words carefully, "we are all very good policemen. That's why we wear the armor. If someone *were* to shoot at us, this stuff *right here* will keep us safe."

"What if they shoot you in the head or leg?"

I had no answer for that, and in the years to come I would also find that I was not alone with my problem.

"My youngest son climbs up in my lap now and checks to see if I'm wearing my vest," Steve Hensley said. "The other night he noticed that I had taken the steel trauma plate out. He demanded that I put it back. A child his age shouldn't be worrying about things like that."

"I know," I agreed. "For a long time after Paris found out what my vest was for, he'd sneak in in the morning to see if I made it home before he went to school. If he doesn't see

me put the vest on, he'll reach up and feel for it as I kiss
him good-bye. A lot of times—on hot muggy evenings—I
would have left it at home if I hadn't known he would
check."

"I see sometimes," Steve said, "just what this job is
doing to our kids. It makes me wonder if it's worth it."

"I know. I know."

"Daddy," the little girl said, "a man in a truck
just stopped. He said you put him in jail and he's gonna *get*
you. He won't, will he?" She was about nine. The other
daughter, two years older, was also standing by, eyes wide
and frightened.

"Where did this happen?" the off-duty cop asked, walking toward the door. He had not lived in the neighborhood
long.

"Down at the gate," the younger child answered.

"What color was the truck?"

"Red and rusty," the older one said. "It went to the dead
end."

"Is that it?" he asked, pointing down to the cul-de-sac.

"Yes," the younger one replied. "He's not gonna get you,
is he?"

"No," he answered. "You two go in the house."

Stepping into the street, he stood trembling with rage.
No pistol, no radio, no back-up—he was no policeman at
that moment. He was a father whose children had been
frightened. The truck came slowly down the street.

When the truck came close enough, he saw a shaggy man
in his early twenties, blond with a scraggly beard. A cigarette dangled arrogantly from his mouth. Looking up, he
spotted the off-duty cop. His eyes opened wide and he tried
to drive around him. The cop did not budge.

Before the truck had come to a complete halt, the cop
dragged him out by the hair, forced him to his knees, and
grasped his throat by the left hand, holding the man's hair
with his right.

"You just scared my daughters," he hissed into his face.

"It wasn't me, I didn't . . . hey! I can't breathe!"

"Don't lie to me! Kids don't make up things like that. *Why did you scare my daughters?* Tell me or you'll leave here under a sheet!"

"I saw the cruiser," he began to sob. "I was just kiddin'."

"You saw the cruiser and decided to scare two little girls, because you're not man enough to face their father!"

"I'm sorry." The man was weeping openly. "It was a joke, honest!"

"It wasn't *funny!*" The officer reached down, took the man's wallet, and flipped it open. He read the license, still grasping him by the throat.

"Now, scumbag, do you know me?"

"No, sir."

"Any cop's kid would have done, right? Answer me!"

"Yes, sir." Tears were running into his scraggly beard.

"You hate cops because they're everything you'll never be. You're worthless, right?"

"Yes, sir." The man was looking at the ground.

"Well, I know who *you* are now, scumbag. You're going to drive away and never come back. If you come into this subdivision again, I'll break your back. If I spend the rest of my life in the penitentiary, it won't matter. Don't come around my family again. *Do you understand?*"

"Yes sir. I understand."

"Get out of here!" He hurled the man away from him. The man crawled to the truck, weeping loudly, and drove away.

As the cop walked back to his house, the rage subsiding, he saw his daughters watching from the window with wide eyes.

They had learned two lessons that day: there are bad people who hate cops, and when the occasion arose, their father could be as bad as any of them.

After all, you do not send a cocker spaniel after a wolf; you send a pit bull.

"Dad," Paris's eyes were wide, "they just said on the television that Officer Wooldridge killed a man. Is it true? Did Bobby kill somebody?"

At eight, he still had blue-brown eyes, blond hair, and a dark Hispanic complexion from his mother's Colombian ancestry. I had meant to tell him before he heard somewhere else, but the moment had not seemed right.

Bob Wooldridge, a Knoxville police officer, is Paris's playmate. They roughhouse whenever Bob comes around for a visit. Bob brings him presents. I do not know which of them enjoys it more.

"Come in here, Hoss. Let's talk."

"Did Bobby kill a man? Did he?"

We sat down on the couch, my son and I. He stared up at me, hoping there was a mistake. One's playmates do not kill people.

"Last night Bob got a call about a man acting very strangely. He was frightening people. The man was very sick, up here." I tapped my head. "When Bob tried to talk to him, he picked up a steel fence post and ran at Bob, trying to hurt him. Bob tried to get him to put it down, but he wouldn't listen. Bob had to shoot him, and he died."

"Like in the movies?"

"No, son. Not like in the movies. It's not like the movies at all. In the movies, people get back up after they die. In real life, that doesn't happen."

"When will we see Bobby again?" Paris is the only person who calls him "Bobby."

"I don't know. Bob feels pretty bad right now. It's hard to shoot someone. But he did what he had to do."

Paris went on his way and did not bring up the subject again. I thought he had forgotten it until we were watching a television show one night. The son of an FBI agent in the television movie asked his father if he had ever shot anyone.

"No," the television agent said. "I've been lucky."

"Dad, Bobby wasn't so lucky, was he?" Paris asked.

"No, son, he wasn't."

★ ★ ★

"Dad, do cops put little kids in jail?"

"No, Paris. Cops never put little kids in jail. If they need protection, we have special shelters for them—never jail. Why?"

"Somebody said if we weren't good, cops would throw us in jail. He said his parents told him."

"Maybe he misunderstood. If not, it was a very ignorant thing for a grown person to say."

He seemed satisfied, but it would get worse, I knew. Cops' kids always catch flack, eventually.

At eight, Paris is still proud to say that I am a cop. "My daddy puts *bad* guys in jail," he tells anyone who will listen. Later, it will be different, because he will know he is different. It happened with both my girls, Kristi and Elaine.

"Watch what you say. The cop's kid will tell on you."

"Did you hear about the cops that beat up . . . ?"

"Does your father carry that gun *everywhere*?"

It grows tiresome. Eventually, they come to resent being singled out, then they feel guilty. When their mother sits by the phone after the news of an injured cop hits the airwaves, the child feels guilty. Hearing sirens in the night after an argument with a forceful and often autocratic cop/parent, they feel guilty.

Other families go to picnics and outings to the lake. If there is unpleasantness, other fathers ignore it. *Theirs* have to play police. Instead of ignoring what happens, the police officer takes command and removes the unpleasantness. Their father never goes off duty.

All the friends with "regular" parents can plan social events on weekends and in the evenings. The cop's kid must have a schedule that usually covers an entire year just to see if it is feasible.

Probably the hardest part is seeing your father publicly accused of brutality, or other wrongdoing, in the newspaper. Everyone seems to read *that*, even if they never read anything else. When the officer is cleared, there will be a few lines buried deep in the paper. Few will see—they will not mention it, even if they do.

In the Book of Ezekiel, the Lord thunders out the question: "What do you mean by repeating this proverb. . . . 'The fathers have eaten sour grapes and the children's teeth are set on edge?'"

I know what it means.

My children did not choose to fight this war in which I am engaged. They were conscripted. Very often, though, they catch the fallout from the skirmishes.

I ate the sour grapes, but it's my children's teeth that are set on edge.

—16—

A Mind Is a Terrible
Thing to Waste

"A MIND IS A TERRIBLE thing to waste," a television public service commercial intones. The commercial refers to potential black students who are financially unable to attend college.

I can never hear the slogan without thinking of Alonzo Smelcer, who was white, a lawyer and a Rhodes Scholar. This is not his real name because I do not know if Alonzo has living family.

He first came into my acquaintance before I was a cop. It was winter 1979, and I was security supervisor at the City-County Building in Knoxville. My job was to oversee twelve guards in the newly opened building. At the time the building was occupied only by the sheriff's department. All city and county offices, however, were in the process of moving from their old homes to a central location in downtown Knoxville.

My employment as security supervisor was what eventually led me into law enforcement. At the time, though, I saw it as only a stopping off point in my journey to literary fame and fortune.

The old courthouse finally closed down when the county clerk's office moved to its new headquarters. Along with the "official" courthouse employees came a couple of others who had been there as long as most of the employees.

There was "Marrying Sam," who was actually a bishop entitled to be called "the Right Reverend," of a church that no longer even had a congregation in the area. He earned his living by performing weddings in the lobby of the old courthouse, then at the front door of the City-County building. He was at his post, wearing a tattered suit and carrying a worn Bible, come rain, sleet, or snow.

A large number of couples in Knox County said their vows before the bishop. He asked no questions, made no distinctions about race, creed, color, or previous condition of servitude. The money was all green.

Along with the bishop came Alonzo Smelcer, who at one time held the record for public drunkenness arrests in Knox County.

Alonzo and the bishop would sometimes talk in the early hours when Alonzo was still sober and when the bishop had no rush ceremonies. They made an interesting pair—the fallen preacher, his vision lost somewhere in the mists of the past, and the fallen lawyer whose only goal was to sink into mindless oblivion.

In the early morning hours, after he had been released from jail and had gone home to change clothes, Alonzo would be impeccably dressed, usually in a dark suit. His shoes would be shined, his white shirt spotless, and his snowy hair combed neatly. His ties lent a splash of color, sometimes with a matching handkerchief peeking out. He carried his dignity of the early morning hours quietly. In a sober condition, it would not have occurred to anyone to call him anything but "sir."

Unfortunately, as Alonzo's level of intoxication rose, his dignity departed him. In my first encounter with him, he was shouting obscenities at a group of school children who were touring the newly opened building.

"Heathens! Swishy, long-haired little bastards! Crumb-grabbers! Rug rats!" He slammed his cane on the floor to emphasize each new name.

"Sir, you are going to have to leave. We can't have you talking like this in a public place."

"Is that so? Have *you*, sir, been informed of the Bill of Rights, which guarantees, among other things, freedom of speech?"

"Have you ever heard it said that your freedom to extend your fist ends where my nose begins, or that freedom of speech does not give you the right to yell 'fire' in a crowded theater?" I inquired quietly.

"By God, a storm trooper with pretensions at education!" He cracked me across the shins with his cane, bringing tears to my eyes.

I grabbed him by the arm to lift him up, aware that I had a huge audience. He promptly grabbed me by the collar and attempted to throw me to the floor. He was incredibly strong for an old man.

Moments later, help arrived. My partner and I grappled with him down the long hallway leading to Main Street. By turns he would go limp, forcing us to carry his two hundred pounds, then erupt in a flurry of punching, kicking, and cursing.

By the time the city police arrived to take him into custody, both Alonzo's fresh attire and our uniforms were in sad condition. He was shouting threats of lawsuit as the car pulled away.

Two days later, he was once more immaculately attired when he showed up. This time he had moved up a floor above the mezzanine where the bishop performed his ceremonies.

"You'd better go on up and have a look at Alonzo," the guard monitoring the building's security cameras said. "He's sitting in front of the coffee shop. He's made a couple of trips to the rest room, so he's already on the sauce this morning."

Most of the guards knew him better than I did. Prior to becoming supervisor, I had worked nights by preference.

"Good morning, Mr. Smelcer," I said as I approached him.

"Good morning, sir. I do believe I created a bit of a disturbance day before yesterday. You have my apology."

"That's good. Then I can depend on you not to verbally or physically attack the people in this building today?"

"I shall keep my medicine to a minimum level, sir."

"What medicine is that?"

"Why, John Barleycorn for what ails you," he replied. "I prescribe it for myself."

"It really doesn't seem to be helping you much," I said.

"Ah, you have researched me, I see. You have no doubt learned how a simple lad worked his way up from the hollows of Claiborne County to become a Rhodes Scholar and a brilliant lawyer with wealth and status, then pissed it all away after his wife died."

"Something like that," I answered.

"Part urban myth, part truth. The real fact, sir, is that the pain of being sober outweighs the humiliation of being a drunk. So I stay drunk when I can. I have an arrangement that allows me to bail out of jail with a minimum of trouble.

"In truth, I was once a school teacher in Claiborne County. That's why I hate children."

"My mother was raised in Claiborne County."

"Really? What was her name?"

"Helen Goin."

"Oh, yes. Helen was one of my students. The Goins were a nice bunch of people. How's your grandfather—Dick, they called him, I believe? And your grandmother. Cassie, wasn't it?"

"My grandparents have been dead a long time. Your memory is amazing."

"Remember, young man. I'm an urban legend. If you'll excuse me, I have to answer nature's call."

I watched him laboriously head for the rest room, vowing to keep an eye on him so that I could remove him before he became obnoxious.

Unfortunately, I got busy.

"Base to Security 1. Head down to the first floor. Alonzo has made *several* trips to the rest room, and he's eyeing that religious delegation on a tour of the building."

"Ten-four," I replied, rushing to the elevator. The delegation was composed of religious leaders of every persuasion. Most were in formal regalia. There were Protestant ministers, Roman Catholic and Orthodox priests, rabbis, and for all I remember, maybe Buddhist monks and Islamic imams.

By the time I arrived, it was too late.

Alonzo was tugging at the sleeve of a rabbi as the group walked by. The man had stopped, a half smile on his face—the kind of expression you give when accosted by drunks, the feeble-minded, or really small children.

"Sir, I see by your name tag that you are of the Hebrew nation."

"Yes, I'm Jewish," the rabbi smiled, nervously. I stopped, holding my breath and hoping for the best.

"I, sir, was a colonel in the Army of the United States until I discovered what the Nazis had done to your people."

I relaxed a little—too soon.

"Yes?" The rabbi had a perplexed smile on his lips.

"It was at that point when I resigned my commission because I knew I was on the *wrong* damn side!" Alonzo thundered, still holding the rabbi's sleeve.

All the religious leaders took a collective deep breath. Their guide had a horrible expression. I moved quickly.

"Gentlemen, if you'll move right along, I'll have Mr. Smelcer escorted out. Thank you." I firmly removed Alonzo's hand from the rabbi's sleeve. The group walked away, murmuring among themselves.

"Alonzo, I cannot believe that a man of your education is a bigot," I said as I escorted him to the street.

"I am *not* a bigot," he said with alcohol-saturated breath.

"Then why did you say what you did to that rabbi?"

"I was merely trying to stimulate a discussion. Far too many people accept things at face value. They need to be shaken up from time to time. Such debates are customary among Jewish scholars. Of course, I can see how he might have thought I was serious," he said.

That was the last time I arrested Alonzo in my official capacity as the security supervisor. My life was approaching a change in direction. Soon afterward, I went into law enforcement as an officer with the Knox County Sheriff's Department.

Alonzo's life had also taken a turn, though it would be a while before I knew about it. He was no longer being arrested on the streets or at the City-County Building. He was being arrested in churches all over town and sometimes at the public library.

He was in search of enlightenment.

It was more than a year after our first encounter. Alonzo was sitting at the booking table, managing to appear aristocratic, even among the weekend crowd of drunken prisoners. His hair was neatly combed as he waited to get out of jail.

Although Alonzo was usually arrested by the Knoxville Police Department, he always was released by the sheriff's department. It was a matter of convenience—for him, not law enforcement.

Ordinarily, a public drunkenness charge (unless there are extenuating circumstances) results in a sentence of "time served." A prisoner can plead guilty, be sentenced to however many hours he has served, then be released from the *city* jail.

Alonzo didn't mind the conviction, but it was six or eight blocks back over to a cab stand. Rather than walk that distance, he would act as his own attorney and send his case to the grand jury. That meant that the sheriff's department had to transport him back over to the *county* jail—just across the street from the cab stand—then release him on bond.

It took a year sometimes for his case to find its way to criminal court, where he would plead guilty and get "time served." Once in a while, a judge would get angry and lock him up for a few days, but most were loath to lock up a man pushing eighty, who once had also been a respectable lawyer.

"Hello, Mr. Smelcer," I said.

He turned and looked at me closely.

"Ah, I see you have become a municipal officer. Was the private sector too dull?"

"Something like that." I emptied his property bag on the table. "I see you're still coming to jail a lot."

"Yes, and it is a travesty of justice—a violation of numerous constitutional rights, including the right of free speech and the right to freedom of religion."

"How's that, Mr. Smelcer?"

"I have been trying for some months now to point out to the local Pharisees and Sadducees who masquerade as followers of the Nazarene that they have fallen far from the path of primitive Christianity."

"They don't want to listen, huh?"

"To the contrary, every time I stand up in their steeple-houses to correct them, I am arrested and persecuted— much like George Fox, the founder of the Quakers."

"I think probably that George Fox was sober when he tried to preach. He was persecuted for heresy, not public drunkenness," I replied.

"Drunk or sober, I see more clearly than they do. The

poor sleep in the doorways of their temples. It's an abomination!"

"Try the Salvation Army," I told him. "They seem to have arrived at a nice balance between the spiritual and the physical man."

"I did. They insist upon sobriety, which, as you know, is beyond my capabilities."

To my knowledge, there was no happy ending to Alonzo's story, no dramatic Damascus Road experience, not even the kind of conversion you hear about at Salvation Army services.

He never stopped drinking "John Barleycorn" as a treatment for his pain, whatever it was. Moving on to the streets, I lost track of him—until I saw his obituary a few years later.

The small block of print devoted to his life and death said that he was formerly a lawyer. There was nothing about the ninety public drunkenness charges still pending. And there was no mention of the torment, whatever it was, that drove a brilliant man to fritter away his existence.

There was no mention of his search for enlightenment— salvation, if you wish.

I like to think that Alonzo stepped across the void of the mystery facing us all and smiled into the face of a God more merciful than we who claim to follow Him.

Still . . . a mind is a terrible thing to waste.

— 17 —

Excuse Me While I Make This Arrest

I WHEELED UP IN FRONT of the department store feeling extremely sorry for myself. Store security had a shoplifter in custody, and I had been sent to transport the prisoner to jail where the security officer would sign a warrant.

The heavy downtown traffic I would have to face at that time of day was only part of the reason for my self-pity. Transporting shoplifters is not an exciting event, especially at that particular store.

Patrol officers had nicknamed the security officer "Wild Bill Hickok." He showed no mercy, ever. It was his option to sign a criminal citation if he wanted, allowing the suspect to report to jail for prints and photographs later. He always insisted on physical custody, however. He and I had once engaged in a heated discussion when he insisted that I transport a mentally retarded girl to jail for the theft of a pair of earrings costing less than a dollar.

Customers paused at the racks to stare curiously as I made my way to the back of the store. Walking through a department store in the afternoon, replete with leather, nightstick, and other paraphernalia, makes a cop feel conspicuous.

In the storage area, Wild Bill Hickok was leaning against the door, smirking as if he had just arrested someone off the FBI's Ten Most Wanted list.

"He tried to walk out of the store with a chainsaw," the security officer said smugly. "I got a *real* professional this time."

"For a change," I said.

The shoplifter sat in a chair, looking nervous. He was about twenty-five with sandy-blond hair. Neatly dressed in a sports shirt and slacks, he looked like the All-American boy. It is the perfect look for a professional shoplifter.

"All right," I told him, "stand up and put your hands behind your back, palms out."

"You're gonna cuff me on a shoplifting charge?" His accent had the broad vowels of Ohio farming country.

"Yep. Everybody who rides in the back of my car goes cuffed. It saves a lot of trouble for everyone."

"There's no need. I'm peaceful."

"*Now* you're peaceful. You may change your mind when we get outside. Put your hands behind your back. I don't feel like wrestling."

He bolted past me without warning, slammed into Wild Bill Hickok, who was covering the door, and ran through the swinging doors leading to the main sales floor.

The security officer was recovering his balance when *I* slammed into him on the way out.

The prisoner had about a twenty-foot head start, so I cut directly through the racks of clothing, rather than around, emerging in front of him a moment later. He turned right at the toy department, just as I rammed into him with my shoulder.

We went down in a pile of crashing figurines. Batman, G.I. Joe, and Masters of the Universe creatures flew everywhere. I caught him by the ankle as he crawled away, but he managed to regain his footing.

Off we went again, through hardware, auto parts, sporting goods, and shoes. A woman carrying several dresses was about to enter a dressing room, but the suspect charged ahead of her. She stepped back startled as I leaped forward and grabbed his shirt.

As the two of us fell forward, the shoplifter grabbed at a curtain. There was a ripping sound as the curtain came down, revealing a tall, regal, and nude woman of thirty or so, poised on one leg, about to step into a bathing suit. Several more suits hung behind her.

My prisoner ceased struggling, entranced by the vision of loveliness that had appeared in front of us. She dropped her foot to the floor and stared back coolly with no sign of panic.

It took *me* a moment to recover, but I quickly handcuffed the prisoner, who had ceased to struggle.

"Excuse me," I said, turning the prisoner to leave. The woman nodded nonchalantly and went back to putting on the bathing suit as if unaware of her appreciative audience.

Outside, I put the prisoner in my cruiser and pulled out. After a few minutes, he sighed deeply.

"Wow. That was almost worth going to jail for."

I did not answer.

"You know," he said, "I always thought they had to wear underclothes when they tried on bathing suits. You know, because of health reasons."

The thought jarred me for a moment. "I believe you're right," I answered.

"Well, *I* ain't gonna complain. That's for sure."

I didn't complain either. Nor did I charge him with trying to escape.

David Shift ("D" detachment) officers of the Knox County Sheriff's Department were answering a burglary in progress late one night. The suspect had fled on foot, and cars had fanned out to search the area.

"I see him," a voice crackled over the airways. "He just went into the back of a trailer."

Moments later, David Shift officers had surrounded the trailer. Officers in place, Sergeant Bob Sexton, the on-scene supervisor, approached the door. As he reached forward, the door opened. Both he and the middle-aged woman stepped back startled.

"What's going on here?" she asked, looking at the officers.

"We need the burglary suspect who just went through the back door of your trailer," Sexton said.

"There's nobody here but me and my mother," the woman answered.

"An officer *saw* him go in," Sergeant Sexton said.

The woman stepped out of the way and motioned the officers in. They moved slowly down the hall, checking the dark places. Finally, they arrived at the end of the trailer.

Standing to both sides, they covered what seemed to be a bathroom door and jerked it open.

A very old woman sat on the toilet, metal walker in front of her. Her eyes were wide as she looked at the officers. Plastered to the wall beside her was the burglary suspect.

Moments later, the officers and the suspect were grappling on the floor as they cuffed him. The old woman sat watching, unmoving and unspeaking, eyes opened wide.

There is nothing funny about having your home invaded by a stranger, especially when he invades your bathroom.

Being the professionals that they are, the David Shift officers maintained straight faces until they left the residence. When they were alone, however, the hysteria set in.

Days later, as Bob Sexton told me the story, both of us were laughing hysterically—not at the burglary or the elderly lady, mind you—but at the incongruity of having a thief and the police engage in battle as you are attending to the most personal needs.

Or maybe cops just have a warped sense of humor.

Christmas is a good time to pick up fugitives. I know it sounds harsh, but sometimes it's the only chance you have.

I had been stalking a fugitive for months. He had jumped bail on a DUI charge after accusing me of stealing from him during the arrest. Some cases get more personal attention than others. An informant had called to tell me that my fugitive was home for Christmas.

With another patrolman covering the back of the house, I knocked on the front door. It was a modest rancher in a middle-class subdivision. The fugitive's brother lived there, and it was his last listed address.

"Yes?" The freckled young woman stood drying her hands on a dish towel. A redheaded child of six or so stood behind her.

"I have a warrant for Joe Tidwell [fictitious name], and I have reason to believe he's here."

"No, I have no idea where my brother-in-law is, but I'll call if he shows up," the young woman replied.

"Momma," the little boy said, "you *know* where Uncle Joe is. He's right over there at the party." The little boy stepped out and pointed at a brick house two doors down.

"Thanks," I said to the little boy. "You're setting a very good example for your mother."

A couple of minutes later, I was at the front door of the brick house. I knocked several times before a middle-aged man responded. He was flushed and jolly and had a glass of wine in his hand. The house was packed with people, and Christmas carols blasted the air.

"Did someone complain about the music, officer? I'll turn it down if they did."

"No, sir, I'm looking for Joe Tidwell."

"Oh," he looked relieved, "a friend of Joe's. Well come right on in. We're tryin' to find him right now. He has a phone call. Feel free to help yourself. Look around, have something to drink."

I had no doubt who was at the other end of the line. It

was a useless call on her part, though, as it turned out. My fugitive had seen the cruisers before she called.

He was nowhere in sight, so I walked down a long hall-way, pushing my way through the crowd. Several people were talking in what appeared to be the master bedroom. They looked up curiously as I entered.

"I'm looking for Joe Tidwell."

"In there," said a girl holding a long-stemmed wine glass. She pointed to the bathroom door.

He was standing in the bathtub with the shower curtain closed, pressed against the wall. He was a tall, lanky man of thirty.

"Let's go," I said, unsnapping my cuff case.

He stepped out of the tub, disgust on his face, and turned to be cuffed. It was an old drill for him. He had been arrested many times.

As we left, the host was standing by the door with a fresh glass of wine in his hands. He was still smiling pleasantly.

"I'm sure everything will work out, Joe," he told my prisoner. "And *you* have a merry Christmas, officer."

"Thanks," I replied as we went down the walk.

Movie and television cops are always involved in exciting and glamorous arrests. The suspect is always dangerous and crafty. Real life cops know better. The glamorous spots are few and far between.

Most fugitives are ready to be arrested. Running and hiding is not pleasant. Capture is generally a relief. Few persons being arrested, however, are as cool and collected as a businessman I picked up a few years ago.

The man's business was what some might call "fly-by-night" if they were being charitable. There were high profits, but also long dry periods when the cash flow was small.

His receptionist did not inquire as to why a uniformed officer was looking for her boss. She pointed me to an office.

The man glanced up as I entered but did not speak to

me. He was dictating to his secretary. He was definitely prosperous looking, in a used-car salesman sort of way.

". . . end it, 'Sincerely yours, etc.' Put it on the special letterhead."

I took out my cuffs. "Excuse me, while I make this arrest." I stepped around the secretary who was busily finishing up the dictation and motioned for the man to stand up and turn around.

"Get reservations for the Atlanta conference," he told her as the ratchets closed on his wrist.

She was still carefully taking notes.

"Oh, yeah, and you'd better call the bail bondsman. I have a dinner appointment tonight."

Not like the movies at all.

—18—

Close Encounters of Another Kind

*I*N MY FIRST book, *The Moon Is Always Full*, I talked about creatures of the animal kingdom that often turn up on a rural police beat. Some of my friends felt that I was less than candid because I looked pretty good in most of the incidents. My old patrol shift members knew that there were a few in which I came out looking less than heroic. For the gratification of my old shift mates and for a cleansing of the soul, I will recount some of these incidents.

My encounters with nonhuman creatures go back much further than my police career. When I was ten years old, my father built a house in a rural area and moved us out of a neighborhood that might charitably be called economically deprived. If you wanted to be less charitable, you would call it a slum. We lived near a train yard and a plant that produced a horrible-smelling chemical. Until I was six years old, I thought all the soil in the world was covered by a layer of black soot.

The new neighborhood was like paradise. The air was clean; there was little traffic; and I was surrounded by woodlands on all sides. For a boy of ten who was enthralled with the legends of mountain men and frontier heroes, it was like going to heaven.

That year I received an air rifle for Christmas, and I *became* a mountain man and a frontier hero. My father was not much of a sportsman, but most of my neighbors were. I was soon tagging along on hunting excursions and, by the time I was eleven, could field dress small game as well as anyone. At the age of thirteen, my father presented me with a twenty-gauge Winchester shotgun. Before the year was out, I was stalking game on my own, without adult supervision.

I also had a dog to help me in my hunting forays. Almost all local hunters had a dog for squirrel and rabbit hunting. They were called "feist dogs" (presumably a derivative of the word "feisty"). These dogs were usually small and of unknown ancestry. My small dog, named "Little Bit," looked like a miniature collie. Little Bit had not been formally trained but had learned his art by following other groups of hunters. I never knew of anyone "training" such a dog. They just absorbed their skills.

Little Bit would flush rabbits from a briar patch or other warren, then stay out of the line of fire as the cottontail darted away. On a squirrel hunt, I would take up a position where squirrels could be found, and Little Bit would circle behind the tree and bark a couple of times. Not noted for its massive intellect or long memory, the squirrel would slip around behind the tree to get out of the dog's line of sight. This maneuver, of course, brought him right into my line of fire. When the bushytail hit the ground, Little Bit would scoop it up and bring it to me. His reward for a job well done was a dog's gourmet delight—the head and entrails.

Early one bitter cold December morning when I was about fourteen, I was ready to head home, having had no luck at all. Just as I was about to leave my hillside position, Little Bit barked, sending a squirrel around the side of a big oak tree. It was a monstrous squirrel—a granddaddy squirrel, one to stuff and hang on the wall. Even from twenty-five yards I could see that it was not a gray squirrel, commonly found around Knox County, but a red fox squirrel, bigger and faster than their less well-endowed brethren.

I snapped off a shot from the Winchester, and the squirrel tumbled down. Little Bit immediately trotted over and snapped it up. Unfortunately, the squirrel was only stunned, not fatally wounded.

Finding a squirrel attached to the end of his snout, Little Bit screamed in canine terror. A squirrel's teeth are long and sharp, designed to cut through a hickory nut like a knife through hot butter. The squirrel had locked onto the dog's nose and upper lip, and he danced around, whining and trying to shake the animal loose.

I quickly ran to the dog's rescue and slammed the butt of my shotgun down on the squirrel. It turned the dog loose and began to chew its way up my shotgun, then up my arm. Before long, I was doing a good imitation of the dog! The squirrel left teeth prints on the stock of my shotgun and on the sleeve of my jacket.

Fortunately, I was heavily clothed. Whirling like a dervish, I shook the squirrel loose as it climbed on the hood of my pullover jersey, and it hit the ground running. Little Bit grabbed it again, and the squirrel immediately sunk its teeth in the dog's lower jaw.

It had become a matter of honor. Picking up a tree branch, I measured the distance and whacked the squirrel squarely. It dropped and lay still. I stood gasping for breath as Little Bit licked at the blood flowing from his jaw and nose.

"Well, it was a game fighter," I told the dog, "but it was its last battle."

I was wrong.

Picking up the squirrel, I stuffed him in the big hand-warming pocket on the front of my pullover. Years later, I would know that doctors sometimes miss signs of life in human beings, so it was not unusual that I had made an inaccurate pronouncement of death on a squirrel.

The totally enraged squirrel came alive inside the front of my shirt. Terror overcame me as I fantasized about the beast clawing its way through my belly. Whirling and yelling, I jerked the pullover off and threw it away from me. Moments later, the squirrel clawed its way out and ran away. Neither I nor the dog made an effort to stop it.

Discretion *is* the better part of valor. That squirrel *deserved* to live.

You would imagine that such a lesson would be sufficient for a lifetime. More than twenty years later, however, while patrolling north Knox County, I made virtually the same mistake.

It was a slow shift, and slow shifts sometimes cause cops to go out and look for something interesting. In this particular incident, I saw an enormous 'possum waddle across the road, into a gravel parking lot.

For the uninitiated and Yankees who might be reading this book, a 'possum is the same creature you know as an "opossum." It is a marsupial, or pouched, animal that resembles a giant, obese rat, with fawn-colored fur. It has a long, hairless tail, with which it can hang from tree limbs. It also has a perpetually runny nose.

When you see the number of 'possums killed on southern highways, you wonder how enough of them survive to perpetuate the species. They are incredibly stupid, and generally wait until a car is too close to dodge them before they run (or waddle) into its path. Also, they have an unusual survival trait. When frightened, they play dead, or "play 'possum," as it were.

I will probably never know what possessed me to do what I did. I decided to capture the 'possum. A less mature policeman might have had it in the back of his mind to put the animal into someone's cruiser at the service center, but I am certain that was not the case with me.

I had a burlap bag in the trunk, in which I had transported some evidence. Following the 'possum onto the large gravel lot, I hit it with my spotlight, and it immediately stopped. Getting out of the car and taking my night-stick, I approached. Darrel Evans, our resident 'possum hunter, had once explained in great detail how to capture a 'possum.

"Just smack 'em with a stick, and they'll fall right over and play dead. Then pick 'em up by the tail. Be sure and wear gloves, they sometimes panic when you pick 'em up. You don't even have to hit 'em hard enough to hurt 'em."

I tapped the large 'possum on the side with my baton. It did not fall over, but turned and *hissed*. I had no idea that 'possums hissed. Deciding that I had a stubborn one, I whacked it a little harder. It was then that the 'possum did something else totally unexpected. It reared up on its hind legs and *lunged* at me, hissing even louder.

Only then did I see the teeth, long and curved, in the light from my cruiser. I fended it off with my baton as it lunged again. It very nearly got past the baton, which I dropped as I took to my heels toward the cruiser.

I jumped up on the hood, pulling my legs out of range. The 'possum stood up on the side of the car, attempting to get at me. I prayed fervently that no cars would come by and find me on the hood of my cruiser, being held at bay by a 'possum that had never learned proper 'possum behavior.

Shooting the animal was never a serious consideration. It was, after all, my fault. The 'possum had been minding its own business. Besides, if I fired the weapon, I might end up filling out a firearms usage report. It would mean making public the humiliating incident.

Eventually, the 'possum went about its business, snuffling as it went, to do whatever they do when they are not chasing cops.

I met the goat early one morning while ranging the back roads of my beat. Morning shift is usually relatively quiet for a patrolman, unless it is raining. Sipping a cup of coffee, I topped a hill near the dead end of a back road.

It was a big billy (male) goat, with a large rack of curved horns and a long flowing beard (a goatee). He was staked out beside the road. Goats are thorough and efficient mowing machines, often used to keep grass down. This one was at the end of his chain, lying in a patch of sunlight on the asphalt. He got up slowly as I approached and walked to the side of the road.

He watched me as I reached the dead end and turned around, then waited for me to come back through. I killed the engine and stopped. After a few moments, he went back to his sunny spot and got comfortable. I started the engine. The goat looked at me and slowly got up again, moving out of the road.

Topping the hill, out of his sight, I turned the cruiser around. Giving him about five minutes to relax, I drove back over the hill. The goat gazed at me for a moment, then got up and moved to the side of the road. I drove by and repeated the process, curious as to how long the goat would go on before giving up.

It was the fourth trip when I finally exhausted his patience. As I drove toward the dead end, the goat backed up and slammed into the side of the cruiser. Startled, I speeded up to get out of range. The big billy goat did *not* lie down, but stood beside the road, pawing the ground, waiting. I understood how the troll felt in "The Three Billy Goats Gruff." That big goat was *serious*.

This time I went by in a hurry, trying to avoid another attack. I had no desire to explain why a goat had beat its brains out against my cruiser. I was not fast enough though. He slammed into the car again as I rushed by. In the rearview mirror, I saw him stagger and recover.

There was no dent on the driver's side of my cruiser, but there was a *distinct* dent on the other side, where he had made the second attack.

A goat's expression is hard to read, but he definitely looked smug as I drove away. I took the cruiser to a body shop and had the dent pulled at my own expense, rather than make a damage report. I had been bested by a billy goat.

Wild critters do not have to be very large to wreak havoc. It happens that I am phobic about spiders. I *know* that most spiders are harmless, but a phobia is not rational. A phobia induces sheer terror. In the military, for instance, I often saw battle-trained soldiers collapse when confronted with a tiny needle.

One hot July evening, I made a traffic stop on a country road. Tree limbs almost touched the top of the cruiser. The area was so heavily wooded that it was like driving down a long, green tunnel. A reserve officer was riding with me that night.

After writing the unfortunate suspect a citation for driving without taillights, I recorded the citation on my log sheet. The dome light was still on as I made the notation, lighting up the interior. A movement caught my eye on the reserve officer's sleeve. I looked but at first saw nothing.

The sheriff's department patch is mostly black and yellow, with a small amount of white and a tiny red, white, and blue shield in the center. As I watched closely, the yellow on his patch began to move.

There is a spider, native to Knox County, commonly called the "writing spider" because of the distinct webs that it weaves. Also, folklore says if it spells your name in its web, you will die. In childhood I had often tormented my brother by threatening to say his name in front of a "writing spider." That may be why my brother also has a phobia about spiders.

It is, I am assured, a beneficial spider, consuming many garden pests. It also is a *big* spider, relatively speaking, with a leg span of up to three inches or so. A person so inclined would say that it was beautiful. Its color perfectly matched the black and yellow shoulder patch, rendering it invisible until it moved.

"Spider!" I yelled, bailing out the driver's side door.

"Where?" he screamed, going out the other side. I was unaware that he shared my fear of spiders until that moment.

"On your shoulder!"

He danced into the ditch, slapping at his shoulder, frantically attempting to look down with terror-stricken eyes. As he whirled in my direction, I ran away, having no desire for physical contact.

Finally, exhausted, he stopped. "Is it gone?" he gasped. "Is it gone?"

"I don't see it," I told him, peering closely at his shoulder with my miniature flashlight. "You must have knocked it off."

"*Where* did I knock it off?"

The import of his words sunk in. The spider might very well be waiting in the cruiser to pounce again. We carefully examined the interior with flashlights, then gingerly got back into the cruiser. I had no doubt in my mind that I would wreck my vehicle if the monster spider crawled on my body.

We drove to a shopping center with the lights on inside the cruiser. Finding a hardware store, we bought an insecticide bomb. I locked the cruiser up and set it off.

"It's gonna really stink in there," the reserve officer said.

"I'll live with it," I replied

As it was, I finished the shift, looking before I touched *anything*. I was up early the next morning to give the cruiser a thorough cleaning. With a shudder, I found the spider under my front seat. He was still big, shriveled though he was in death. I set off *another* insecticide bomb to be certain that he had not brought any friends.

Close encounters of another kind are there for the taking. All you need are a few thoughtless moments and a couple of wrong assumptions.

It will be something to tell your grandchildren.

—19—

Divide the Living Child in Two

I PARKED MY CRUISER behind the red sports car, stopping for a brief moment to look at it wistfully. Ownership of such a sports car has been one of my secret ambitions. It remains secret because I have no real expectation of ever owning such a frivolous thing—not on a cop's salary, not while raising a family.

In front of the sports car was a new Cadillac. A Mercedes was parked in front of the Caddy. The house was magnificent. The exterior was done in river stone, and the house was built into the side of a hill. There appeared to be a full story downstairs and two above ground.

I wondered what kind of dispute would cause such obviously prosperous people to call the cops. Generally, people in such neighborhoods will go to any length to keep their neighbors from seeing a police car at the house.

Approaching the door slowly, I listened and looked. A "domestic dispute" can be anything from a loud argument to a fatal encounter. The complainant, I had been informed, lived here.

"Officer?" the carport door opened and a man in his fifties spoke to me. "In here, please."

The man was dressed in slacks and a sweater over a knit pullover. It looked as if perhaps he had been golfing or was about to go. Once inside the house, he introduced me to his wife, who had perfectly styled hair, streaked with a bluish tint where it had turned gray.

"What can I do for you?" I asked.

Before either of them could answer, a young woman of twenty or so stalked into the room and added an armload of clothing to a pile of boxes and suitcases by the door.

"I see you called the police! Well, it *won't* do any good." The young woman was pretty in a plump, pouting way. Not to my taste, but some would have called her beautiful.

She stalked out of the room.

"That's our daughter. She just got out of drug rehabilitation six weeks ago. She's getting ready to take Tammy, our granddaughter, out of here," the woman said, as if her statement explained my presence.

"How old is your daughter?" I asked.

"Barely twenty," the man said, "and Tammy's only a year old."

"Is your daughter drunk or under the influence of drugs?" I asked.

"No, she *has* managed to stay away from *that*. But she sneaked a man into her downstairs apartment last night. We will not put up with that, and she knows it. We told her it would stop, or she could leave."

"It appears that she *is* leaving," I pointed out.

"Yes, but she's taking Tammy with her." Once more the woman sounded as if everything should be clear to me.

"Do you have legal custody of your granddaughter?"

"No," the man said, "but we have provided everything she has while our daughter has wasted her life. Now she brings that, that . . . hoodlum into my house. He has no legal right to be here, even if he is Tammy's father. They were never married," the man said lamely.

"What exactly is it that you expect me to do?" I asked bluntly.

They both looked at me as if they could not believe their ears.

"We expect you to tell her she can't take the baby out of here," the man said. "It's obvious she's not fit to have a child. She doesn't even have anywhere to go."

"I can't do that." I braced for the storm.

"You can't protect a baby? Is that what you're saying?" The woman's voice had become shrill.

"Yes, I can protect babies—when they're in danger. Your daughter is a sober, legal adult. She has a perfect right to take her baby when she leaves."

"I'll go to court," the man growled. "I play golf with judges."

"You do that," I said. "Right now, though, there is absolutely nothing you can do."

The woman started to say something, but her husband raised his hands.

"Look, I didn't mean to throw my weight around. Maybe if you talk to her, she'll listen. She can stay here as long as she wants as long as she stays away from *him*."

"All right." I walked down the hallway where the girl had gone. I found her in a pink bedroom where the bulk of her belongings apparently remained. It looked like a high school girl's room, which it had been only a couple of years earlier.

"Are you going to arrest me?" she snapped as she slammed clothes into a small suitcase.

"No. You don't even have to talk to me, but I'd appreciate it. Sometimes a third party can offer a solution." It was then that I saw the baby sitting quietly in her crib, staring at me with big brown eyes. "You have a beautiful baby."

"Thanks." She pushed a wisp of hair back from her face and relaxed somewhat.

"Parents can be rough. I think there's a law that says we can't communicate with our parents," I said with a smile.

"Oh, we communicate. They tell me what they want, and I'm supposed to do it."

"Do you have anywhere to go?" I asked.

"No, but I'm not staying here another night." She slammed the suitcase closed.

"Does your mother take care of your daughter?"

"Yes, but *I'm* her mother and *Jimmy* is her father. I know they don't want him around. He comes in here, and they never see him unless they're spying like they were last night."

"This *is* their home," I said quietly.

"I *know* that. And I follow their rules, except for Jimmy."

"What's their problem with Jimmy?" I asked.

"He's a bum," she said.

"Pardon?"

"He doesn't work. He's a bum. I know that, but I can't have any other relationships. I work all day, and they don't want me to leave at night."

"How about this," I said. "Leave Tammy here until you find a place. You know she'll be taken care of. It's cold out there. You don't need to be on the streets with a baby."

"No! I'm finished with them." She picked up the baby and walked toward the living room. Opening a closet door, she took out a miniature parka.

"Just stop right there," her mother said. "We paid for all those clothes. We paid for *everything*. Just put that coat right back."

"You're going to send your granddaughter out into this weather without a coat?" the girl snarled, eyes flashing.

"Why not? You're taking her out on the streets. *Everything* stays here except what she's wearing."

"Another thing," her father said. "*I* paid for that fancy sports car of yours. You're not taking it anywhere."

"Yes, I am. It's in my name, *remember*? It was a gift. I might have known it would have strings attached, like everything else you ever gave me!"

"Officer, can she take the car that I paid for?"

"If it's in her name, she can," I said tiredly.

"Fine," the man said. "In that case, get her out of my

house right now. Everything in this house belongs to me, and that includes her clothes and the baby's clothes. She can leave the way she came to us."

"That's great! Your true colors are really shining through," the girl screamed. "You'd put your daughter and granddaughter naked on the streets to get your own way! Mother, are you going to stand there and let him put us out of here without any of our belongings?"

"You made your bed," the chic woman said through compressed lips, "now *lie* in it—or listen to reason."

"Hand me the baby!" I growled, walking toward the girl. Startled, she handed her over.

"What are you doing?" the girl asked.

"I'm taking this child into protective custody. It's obvious that everyone here is more concerned with pride than in seeing that this baby is safe. In my opinion, she's in jeopardy."

I was bluffing, taking a line from King Solomon. "Divide the living child in two," he said during a long ago custody dispute. It worked for him. The real mother was willing to give up the child because she loved it.

"What . . . what will happen to Tammy?" the grandmother asked.

"I'll take her to a shelter and turn her over to the Department of Human Services. She'll go to a foster home until a custody hearing can be held."

I watched their faces, waiting for love to overcome pride, waiting for a compromise.

"Well, at least she won't be around your drug-using friends," the grandmother said.

"You won't have her either!" the daughter snapped back.

"All of you shut up!" I finally said.

"You can't talk like that in my house—" the man began.

"I said shut up! You." I turned to the girl. "Gather up the baby's things, including the coat. I can't stop you from leaving with the baby, and neither can your parents, but the baby is not going out naked. You all disgust me. *All* of you are selfish beyond belief."

The girl's parents stared at the floor as she carried out the baby's things. I kept waiting for a compromise, but none came. I followed her outside and watched her get into the red sports car.

"Here's my card," I said, turning to the parents. "Feel free to complain about my behavior if you wish. Legally, I *did* what I had to. What I *said* was strictly opinion—and I'm not supposed to have an opinion."

Neither of them reached for the card, and I never heard anything else about it.

It was a good plan. It worked for Solomon. Unfortunately, someone has to *really* love the child for this approach to be successful.

And I've never claimed the wisdom of Solomon, just familiarity with his work.

— 20 —

I Demand Action!
I Demand It Now!

*T*HE TIRES ON my cruiser made a crunching sound as I drove up the long, winding driveway to the mobile home that sat on top of one of the many ridges in Knox County. It had been a busy day, and I was tired and disgusted.

I was answering a vandalism call. The complaint clerk had tried to explain to the complainant that sending an officer was pointless. He refused to give her the report by telephone, even after she explained that vandalism is a misdemeanor. His only course of action—if he knew who did it—was to see a judge and obtain a warrant.

The man had insisted on talking personally to an officer. It was his right as a taxpayer.

A man—big bellied, beltless, and barefoot, with blue jeans sagging in the seat—came out of the trailer, a can of Budweiser in his hand. His sandy hair was long and shaggy, as was his beard. He could have been thirty or forty years old.

"It's about time you got here," he said, without preliminaries. "I been waitin' for an hour. And I got better things to do than wait on cops. If you was doin' your job of patrollin', I wouldn't have this problem now."

"What *is* your problem?" I gritted my teeth and swallowed hard, determined not to drive my blood pressure up. Idiots are an occupational hazard of police work.

"Somebody scattered roofin' nails all over my driveway." He took a swig of beer and smiled meaningfully, looking at my cruiser.

"If you had told the complaint clerk that, I wouldn't have driven my car up here," I said.

"Yeah, well the way I see it, that's *your* problem. I didn't like that clerk's attitude. I'm a taxpayer, an' I deserve some service when I been victimized."

An explanation would have been wasted. So I took out my pad and began the report. After I put in the preliminary information, I proceeded with the investigation.

"Do you have any idea who might have done this?"

"I *know* who done it. It was the guy in the house across the road. He's pissed because I damned up the spring to make a pond. He says there ain't enough water gettin' across my property to water his cows."

"Have the two of you discussed it?"

"Nothin' to discuss." He belched and threw the beer can on the ground. "It's *my* property and I do what *I* want with it. Let him dig a well if he needs more water."

"Well, there's no problem. If you saw him do it, a judge will give you a warrant, and we'll arrest him." I put the clipboard back in the car.

"I never *seen* him," the man said.

"If you didn't see it, how do you know it was him?" I asked, certain that there were a long line of people who might have a grudge against him.

"Because that's the way people *are*. Ever'body wants revenge when they've been done wrong."

"I don't know. Maybe he's not as small-minded and vindictive as you are." I got back in the car. It had been beyond my capacity to resist the parting shot.

"I don't know that word, but I know it was a smart-ass remark. I'm gonna call the sheriff!"

"Get a dictionary," I said, leaning out of my cruiser window. "Find somebody who can read, and have them *tell* you what it means."

"You'll keep comin' up here until I get somethin' done," he yelled as I pulled away.

My right rear tire was flat before I got back to the highway, a roofing nail in it.

"Baker 10, see the subject regarding a vandalism . . ."

My face flushed as the dispatcher gave me the same remote address and the same information as before.

"Baker 10. I took that report yesterday. Has there been another vandalism?"

"Negative. The subject says he wants an update on the progress in his case. He demands to see an officer."

"Ten-four," I replied. Then, under a rush of inspiration, "Tell him if he wants to talk to me, he'll have to walk down to the road. I can't take a chance on damaging another tire."

I drove through the darkness of the back country road, not really expecting the man to be at the road. It did not seem likely that his desire to harrass me would extend to walking the long distance down the driveway.

He was made of sterner stuff than I thought, or he was enjoying himself so much that he did not want it to end. As I topped the last hill, I saw him standing by his mailbox, leaning on it for support, another can of beer in his hand. As I slowed, he stepped directly in my path and put up his hand like a traffic cop. He smiled, enjoying himself immensely.

"It took you longer today than it did yes'erday." He was slurring his words, much drunker than the day before. He could not see *me* smiling in the darkness as I approached him.

"What was it you wanted? The complaint clerk says there's nothing new to report."

"I want some *by God* action. *That's* what I want. You'll keep drivin' out here until somethin's done. I demand action, and I demand it *now!*"

"You're absolutely right. Drop the beer can, put your hands on the front of my car, and spread your legs. You're under arrest for being publicly drunk."

He staggered back a step, staring owlishly at me in the headlights. "You can't arrest me on my own property. I know the law."

"You, sir, are on a public road, intoxicated to the point that you walked in front of a moving vehicle. You obviously are in no condition to care for yourself. I'd not only be grief stricken if you came to harm but also liable for any injury to you. Please do as I say, before I have to take physical measures to get you in the car." I was very careful to say "please."

The next day he pleaded guilty to being publicly drunk. Apparently, he worked out the problem with his neighbor. He never demanded to see another officer—not while I worked the beat.

Police switchboards stay lit every day with calls and complaints. All individuals believe their problem is of paramount importance and want service *now.*

Generally, professional complaint clerks are able to sort the calls in order of urgency. Most people merely need to ventilate a little. After a few sympathetic words they calm down. If it is a matter that can be handled by phone, most people are agreeable.

Unfortunately, there are numerous exceptions. Some people see police as a cure-all for every problem. They call about snakes under the house, noisy airplanes, and flooded basements. If the dispatcher knows the proper agency, the call will be forwarded. If not, an officer has to be sent.

The tendency to expect miracles from the police is not

limited to the very young or to the uneducated. One night I found an alarm going off at a high school. The building seemed secure, and the principal was called.

Upon entering the building, we found that the alarm had been caused by an electrical short. A pipe in the sprinkler system had burst, soaking the wiring in a wall.

As we stood watching the water pour from the ceilings, the principal turned to me. This was a man with a master's degree, an educator.

"Well," he said, "are you going to do something or not?"

I explained that I had left all my plumbing tools at home and advised him to contact his maintenance people.

Many calls are from people who really need social workers. Sometimes they do not know any better. More often it happens that people who *do* know better want to use officers as the instrument of revenge.

After an argument, an enraged spouse will often wait until three in the morning, call the police, and say she needs to pick up her belongings and is afraid to go alone. Wake most people up at that time of morning, and you usually *do* have a problem.

Some calls fall in a gray area. They're not really criminal, but nonetheless they call for some type of police action.

One such incident brings a smile to my lips whenever I think of it—not because of the sadness involved, but because of the way it ended.

It came in as a "domestic problem in progress." My reserve officer partner and I carefully looked over the small frame house as we pulled up. It was painted a lemon yellow, and the grass was long. The owner obviously was not worried about what his neighbors thought.

There were lights at the rear of the house, and we knocked at the back. A small, mousey woman with graying hair opened the door. She appeared to be in her mid-thirties.

"Did you call for an officer?"

"No." She bit her lip as if wanting to say more. "But my husband did."

"I'm the one who called." The man appeared from the living room. A lanky man, roughly the same age as his wife, he was wearing a sleeveless T-shirt and blue jeans. A huge silver belt buckle covered almost his entire midsection. There were tattoos up and down both stringily muscled arms. He was wearing a red ball cap inside the house.

"I want my father-in-law out of the house, and he won't leave," the man said.

"He's got nowhere to go," the woman said quietly.

"That's not my problem," the complainant snapped at his wife. "He broke our agreement, and I want him out *now*."

"This sounds like something that can be worked out in the family," I said. "There's been no violence. Why don't you wait until tomorrow? When you cool off things may look different."

"*Look*," the man said, stepping forward, "this is *my* house. If a stranger walked in without permission, you'd take him out of here. It means nothin' to *you* that he's my father-in-law. He ain't got a lease, and I want him out *now*."

"Where is he?" I asked tiredly.

"First door on the right," the complainant said, "and make it quick. I'm missin' a good television program."

The room was dimly lit, hardly more than a cubbyhole. It was neat, however. A small bed, a chair, and a dresser were the only items of furniture. On the wall, hanging from a nail was a leather belt and several wrenches. The wrenches gleamed in the dim light. I recognized the tools immediately. They were ironworker tools.

"I'm Officer Hunter with the sheriff's department," I said to the elderly man occupying the lone chair. His hair was iron gray, the same color as his metal-rimmed glasses, which were taped together in the middle with white tape. His hair was clipped in a crew-cut—the kind popular thirty years ago. He appeared to be in his seventies.

"I heard y'all talkin' down the hall. I ain't deaf, just old."

"I see you were an ironworker," I said, nodding to the tools hanging on the wall.

"Whatta you know about ironwork?" he asked, suspicious.

"Well, my daddy was an ironworker. I did a little connecting and bolting up for a couple of years, up around Middletown and Cincinnati."

"Is your daddy dead or crippled?" he asked.

"He died in 1968 from an injury he got on a job in Ohio," I replied.

"I figgered that. Ain't too many of us live to git old in the ironworkin' business—not unless we git crippled first. You was smart to get into a safer line—like police work."

"You're right," I said. "Ironwork is one of the most hazardous jobs on earth."

"Damn right," he said, "I *used* to think I was one of the lucky ones, but bein' old ain't no picnic."

"What's the problem here tonight?" I asked.

"Money. I give him all my Social Security money ever' month, except for forty dollars. I just broke my glasses, though. I told him I was gonna buy a new pair. He told me to give him the usual amount or git out. A few years ago I woulda broke him in half. I've only stayed because of my daughter. He don't treat her as bad when I'm here."

"Do you have somewhere to go?" I asked.

"I got a son, but he lives outta state. I'll have to git my check cashed before I can go."

"We'll talk to your son-in-law," I said.

In the living room the old man's son-in-law was stretched out in an easy chair, sipping a Coors. Looking across the room, both my partner and I saw the planter at the same time. I punched him before he could say anything.

"We need to talk," I said. "Your father-in-law says he can leave tomorrow."

"He's leavin' *tonight*. Take him to the Salvation Army or

to jail. I don't care. He's not gonna freeload off me any-more."

"What if he gives you the money instead of buying the glasses he needs?"

"If he wants to do that, he can stay." The man took an-other sip of beer. "As long as he knows this is *my* house." It was in the open, at last. He was trying to use us to extort money from the old man.

"Sounds fair enough," I said. "It *is* your house. I'd guess nothing goes on without your permission."

"That's right. I say what goes and what don't. I *paid* for everything here. I *brought in* everything here. I *own* every-thing."

"You've made *that* plain enough," I said, smiling to my partner. "You own everything here: the house, the furniture . . . that planter over there with the five plants in it."

The man whirled, his eyes wide. He looked at the planter, then at me and my smiling partner. He began to stammer.

"I . . . I . . . it was just an *experiment.* I wanted to see if the seeds would grow."

"They certainly did," I said cheerfully. "You must have a green thumb."

"You wouldn't charge me with possession for five crummy little marijuana plants, would you? Be *reasonable.*"

"I always try to be reasonable. I admire a reasonable, compassionate man. I won't charge you with possession." He looked relieved, but only momentarily.

"The charge will be manufacturing for resale. It's a fel-ony. I must advise you that you have the right to remain silent. If you give up the right to remain silent . . . ."

My partner and I tried not to look too pleased as we es-corted the man outside. His wife stood silent as we went through the kitchen.

"Honey," he said plaintively, "bring some money down and bail me out. This is my second offense. There's gonna be a heavy bond on me."

"Sorry," she said, not even trying very hard to look sad, "but I don't have any money."

"Cash your father's check—" he began.

"I can't. He's leavin' in the mornin'. You threw him out, remember? He's gonna go live with John. I'll tell him you said 'bye, though."

At such times in my career I have fully understood the term *poetic justice*.

A good thing to remember is this: when you demand action, sometimes you get it.

— 21 —

It Seemed Reasonable at the Time

*P*ARANOIA IS DEFINED as "a mental disorder characterized by an unwarranted fear of persecution." In other words, if you think people are out to get you and they aren't, you're paranoid. It follows then, if you think people are out to get you and they are, you're being realistic.

Cops walk a thin line between paranoia and reality throughout their careers. An FBI agent addressing a roomful of officers expressed the opinion that most cops think Humpty-Dumpty was pushed. He said some cops avoid football games because they think the players are discussing them in the huddles.

Most of us aren't that bad, but our training and lifestyle are geared to distrust, beginning at the place where cops are trained: the academy.

From day one, budding cops watch films about officers who were careless. It is drummed into them at the academy and at every in-service for the rest of their careers that there are only two kinds of cops: the quick and the dead.

The wonder of it is that cops don't flounder more often

than they do. Men and women who carry badges must make decisions, often in a split second, that will be debated for years by judges and lawyers.

Sometimes cops do and say things that seem reasonable at the time, but . . . .

        The alarm came in from an upper-class neighborhood in an exclusive subdivision where some of the houses adjoined the country club golf course. It was a "silent" alarm, which meant that there was no bell or siren in the house. Such an alarm goes off on a control panel at the security company, which then notifies the police.

The first officer to arrive wheeled into the subdivision, looking for the proper street number. A second cruiser came in behind him. Moments later, the first cruiser pulled into a driveway.

Quietly the officers approached the front door. It was unlocked. Swallowing hard, the first officer slipped in. He was quickly followed by the second officer and his reserve partner.

The most common search patter is a "leap-frog" type movement. The first officer moves in quickly, scans the room, then signals the officer behind him, who moves further in, repeating the action.

"Hold it! Don't move! Police officers!" The first officer yelled, dropping into a shooting crouch.

The two officers behind him approached the door from the sides. In a bedroom, a man and woman were sitting up in bed, wide-eyed, sheets pulled around their necks.

"Who . . . who are you?" the man asked.

"Police. What are you doing in here?" the first officer asked.

"We live here," the man replied.

"The alarm in this house is going off," the officer said.

"That's not possible," the man replied.

"Why not?"

"I turned the alarm off last night because I'm expecting

guests and didn't want to be disturbed. I left the front door unlocked."

"Well," the pistol was still pointed at them, "the alarm is going off."

"That's impossible," the frustrated man snapped.

"Look," the officer was also becoming frustrated at the standoff, "this *is* 7828 Widow's Bend Road [not the real address], *isn't* it?"

"No," the man answered, "it *isn't*."

The two back-up officers were already hurrying to their cruiser, wishing with all their hearts that they had never showed up. Apparently, however, the first officer was a smooth talker, able to calm the irate citizen and convince him that it had been a *reasonable* mistake.

It was about two o'clock in the morning as I cruised down a north Knox County back road. I was yawning, sipping a cup of coffee, and wishing something would break the monotony.

As I approached a three-way intersection, I became aware of an old black Pontiac stopped, with the engine running and the parking lights on. I was westbound; the Pontiac was stopped at the intersection coming from the south.

Slowing down, I reached for my spotlight switch. Cops are naturally nosey.

Suddenly, the Pontiac squalled away from the intersection, burning rubber and heading east past me. It was obvious that my cruiser was the reason for the sudden panic.

I wheeled around at the intersection, hitting my blue-lights and siren. Reckless driving is always a good reason for stopping a suspicious vehicle. Within minutes, I had added "speeding" and "failure to halt for stop signs."

His reason for fleeing quickly outweighed my reason for pursuing. With speeds approaching eighty miles per hour on a secondary road, I terminated. On a felony, I might have pushed it, but not on traffic charges.

A mile or so down the road, I drove up to a man surveying the crushed remains of a black Pontiac, which had come to rest against a concrete wall. I probably was smiling a little as I got out. The air was still filled with the smell of burning rubber, gasoline fumes, and antifreeze.

"Is this your car?" I asked the man.

"Yes, I—" He was young, had long, blond hair, and was wearing jeans and a flannel shirt.

"Has anyone else been driving your car tonight?"

"No, but—"

"Then put your hands on the side of the car and spread your legs real wide," I said.

"Officer, I—"

"Do it, now!"

He quickly complied. I put him in the back of my cruiser and called for a wrecker. He tapped on the window.

"Yes?" I asked, opening the door.

"There's been some sort of mistake here," he said.

"Yes, and *you* made it," I replied, closing the door.

Walking back up the road, I found the point where the skid marks began and paced them back to the scene of impact. As I made notes on my rough draft report, I noticed that the skid marks did not end at the point of impact.

A sinking feeling struck me in the abdomen. Walking to the front of the car, I laid my hand on the hood. It was cold. I followed the skid marks for a hundred feet where they went over an embankment.

Another black Pontiac, identical make and model to the one in the street, had come to rest against a tree. The driver had fled the scene, however—the driver I had been chasing.

"What are the odds?" I wondered aloud, shaking my head as I walked back to my cruiser. "What are the odds that a fleeing black Pontiac would crash into its twin, parked by the road?"

"I owe you an apology," I told the young man as I let him out of the back seat, thanking God that I had not put handcuffs on him. "Walk down here with me, and I'll explain."

"Well, I'll be damned!" he exclaimed upon examining the twin to his car. "I wonder what the odds are of this happening?"

"Beats me," I replied. I was thankful that he was taking it so well.

Jim Wester, a veteran patrol officer with the Knox County Sheriff's Department, was awakened one morning by a strange noise. He had worked the previous night shift and had not hit the bed until after 7:00 A.M. that morning, about two hours earlier.

Opening his eyes slightly and still half asleep, he saw a man standing in the living room, directly in front of his bedroom door. It was a cop's nightmare. From the stranger's hand a tubular device protruded. To a cop with an adrenalin rush, any tubular device translates to a weapon.

Wester is not a man given to panic. Years of handling emergency situations have prepared him to think (however briefly) before acting. A stocky man of medium height, with brown, curly hair, he appears to always be considering options. If he smiles at roll call, he is about to tell a humorous story. If he smiles on the street, he is about to arrest someone whom he deems vastly deserving of such a fate.

The situation in a nutshell (at least to a cop half asleep and rudely awakened) was this: the intruder apparently had not noticed Wester, as his back was partially turned. Wester's weapon was nearby, but he feared that movement and noise would draw attention before he could reach it.

Jim Wester decided that the best defense was an offensive move.

He hurtled from the bed, screaming to disorient his opponent (as he had been taught), and charged at the man who was turning to look. Wester was in his normal sleepwear; he was stark naked. My friendship with Wester goes back a long way; we attended the academy together. From experience with communal showers, I can attest that having him come at you screaming in a stark naked condition would be a frightening affair.

His momentum carried the two of them to the floor, where Wester immediately seized the intruder by the throat with the intention of throttling him into a state of unconciousness. The man, who probably had never been attacked by a naked cop, fought back furiously.

"As I came awake," Jim said, "I noticed that the tube he had been holding was attached to a canister with the name of a pest control company on it. I was choking the pest control man."

The embarrassed officer let go of the terrified technician and went to find his trousers. He gave the man a lecture about why he should never, ever, enter a residence where a police car is parked without first rousing the occupant.

Personally, I doubt that the warning was needed.

The officer was well-groomed for the occasion, and he had practiced the answers to questions that he thought might come up. He was interviewing for an opening in the detective division and was prepared (he thought) as he would ever be.

He had reviewed search and seizure laws, knew the definition of "fruits of a crime," and had even gone back to read case law affecting the job he wanted to do.

It was incomprehensible to him that a question could be thrown at him for which he had not prepared. It happened, though, and the communications breakdown was unbelievable.

"Officer," the assistant chief asked, "have you had any drug experience?" What the interviewer meant, of course, was, "Have you ever worked on narcotics cases?"

Startled by the unexpected question, the officer hesitated for a moment, then blurted out what seemed a perfectly reasonable answer at the time.

"Chief, I'll have to admit that I did smoke a little pot when I was in college, but *nothin'* since then."

The silence, I have been told, became deafening in the room as the officer realized with dismay what he had just said was not as reasonable as it had seemed.

He didn't get the job.

— 22 —

Laugh, Even If It Hurts

MIKE FREEMAN IS a highly dignified man and a respected officer of the Knox County Sheriff's Department, now an investigator. Had it not been for his dignity and respected status, it would not have been nearly as funny the night he fell on his face and couldn't get up.

Sergeant Bob Sexton, then Freeman's supervisor, was delivering a lecture at the time. The lecture concerned waiting for proper back-up before entering a dangerous area.

Mike was listening, properly attentive, hands thrust deep into the pockets of his uniform trousers. He was also rocking back and forth from the balls of his feet to the heels. Somehow he became over-balanced as he went forward. Unable to get his hands out of his pockets, he crashed.

"For a couple of minutes," Sergeant Sexton said, "he thrashed around like a turtle trying to roll over."

It was a great roll call story. Freeman knew it would be repeated until someone did something funnier. Cops are merciless, no matter where you find them.

The call had come in as "burglary of an auto in progress." On a slow night, every car in the vicinity responds to an "in progress" call. There is always the chance, no matter how small, that a thief can be caught in the act.

It was a highly congested area, with cars parked along both sides of the street in an old neighborhood of two-story houses that had been converted into apartments. Many of the apartments were occupied by students of a nearby university.

On the theory that he might have doubled back through an alley, one of the officers responding [let's call him Chad] decided to go to the opposite end of the block to corner him. Midway down the block, someone stepped in front of his cruiser. Locking up the brakes, Chad began to slide. Moments later, he crashed into a classic 1955 car parked by the curb.

At the same moment, an officer down the block announced that he had caught the thief, who was still carrying a tape player he had ripped from a car. Chad got out and walked around to the front of his vehicle.

The damage to the cruiser was minimal. The side of the classic car, however, was scraped from front to back. Fifteen coats of carefully applied lacquer were down to the bare metal. Some things are never quite the same after you damage them.

Chad turned angrily, looking for the individual who had walked in front of his cruiser. Before he could speak, a dark young man, who appeared to be Indian, or at least from somewhere in the region, approached. He was sobbing loudly.

"Why did you walk out in front of me?" the officer demanded to know.

"It was I who called," the man said, tears staining his dark complexion. "It was my car that was burglarized."

Chad thought it over a minute. It was going to be problem enough explaining why he had plowed into a parked vehicle. He decided that a complaint from a citizen would not be a good idea on top of everything else. He decided to get in a little public relations before hunting down the owner of the vehicle he had struck.

"Well, sir, I am happy to report that the police department has recovered your stolen stereo less than five minutes after it was stolen. An officer will bring it up here in a minute. He has the thief in custody."

"Is very good," the man sobbed, sitting down on the curb, head in arms.

"Sir, you should be happy. I know the thief probably broke your vent window to get in, but the insurance will cover it."

"That is not why I'm weeping. The window was a small thing," the man said, wiping tears from his eyes.

"Then what's wrong?" Chad asked.

"Is my 1955 Chevrolet you just crashed into," the victim said with renewed sobbing.

It was just a little after six in the morning. The attendant who opened the service center was running late. Several cruisers were waiting across the street, engines running in the cold winter air.

Settling in, I closed my eyes and apparently drifted into a light sleep. I heard the voice crackling over the car-to-car channel and came awake.

"Hunter, are you gonna get gas or not?" someone asked impatiently.

"Yeah," I replied, apparently not fully awake. I dropped the Ford in gear and shot across the street, where the attendant was in the process of opening the eight-foot gate. He had not gotten it fully open and ran for cover as I knocked it off the hinges and into the service center lot.

Horror washed over me. In front of fifteen officers—with absolutely no excuse—I had hit a fixed object. There was no way I could even make up a plausible story.

With relief, I saw that the damage to my car was almost nonexistent. It could be repaired with a tiny piece of chrome and a little rubbing compound.

As for the gate, a mechanic with the county school systems took pity on me. Together, we got it back on track. There was no noticeable damage. That gave me until Monday, when my reports were read by my boss, to fix my cruiser.

I hoped the chief would be merciful if everything was repaired. The taunts from my comrades in arms went over my head that Saturday morning as I plotted feverishly to save myself. I had one more shift that week, though.

The next morning I was running a little late. As I approached the service center, I did a double-take. Officers were lined up on both sides of the gates with flashlights. At the pumps, the sergeant stood with a traffic wand. Dramatically, he flagged me in, like a controller bringing a jet down on an aircraft carrier.

As I came to a stop, everyone cheered and came by to congratulate me on not hitting the gate. It wasn't over yet. The report still had to be filed for Monday morning.

All day Monday I waited for the call from my boss. No longer able to take the suspense, on Tuesday I went by headquarters. "How upset was the chief?" I asked the lady who handles damage reports.

"You mean about the scratch on your cruiser?"

"Yeah?"

"He hardly looked at it," she replied.

"No kidding?"

"Yeah, after he read Bernie Lyon's report, he was so angry that he just glanced at yours."

"What was in Bernie's report?"

"It said that he was driving down the interstate and an object of unknown type and origin fell out of the sky and knocked his windshield out."

Almost giggling in relief, I left. Bernie's loss was my gain. In battle you hate to see your friends go down, but you're always relieved that it's them and not you.

Bernie Lyon's report of an object of "unknown

type and origin" is not unusual. Neither is it unusual to be run off the road by a mysterious vehicle, usually black or white, when there is no other rational reason to have run off the road. Most people have difficulty admitting that they ran off the road because they had their mind somewhere else.

In addition to an almost paranoid desire for physical safety, all cops practice CYA survival. CYA means "cover your ass." Practitioners of CYA do not consider creative report writing to be falsehood, although others might.

For instance, an officer who hit a dumpster in a parking lot wrote that his vision was "obscured by foggy conditions." He failed to mention that he was also chasing a stray dog around the parking lot, shooting at it with a water pistol when he hit the six-by-eight-foot garbage receptacle.

It becomes ingrained in a cop after a while that he must CYA, cover every angle, explain every minute detail. The "official memo" is as much a part of police work as the gun and the badge.

Sometimes the urge to CYA is so overwhelming that it obscures everything else, including what really happened.

The storm had just ended a few minutes before the cruiser rounded a sharp curve. A section of limb, blown from a tree, was across the road. Before he could brake, the officer hit it.

"Oh, no," the patrolman said in anguish to his reserve partner as he surveyed the damage to his bumper, "it's memo time. We have to CYA here."

"Yeah, I guess so," the reserve officer said, not sure he understood the term.

"All right," the patrolman told him, "here's what we'll say. We were just driving along when all of a sudden these kids ran to the edge of the embankment and hurled this limb in front of us. There was no way we could miss it. How does that sound?"

The reserve officer, who was a civilian and had not lived

in terror of memos for years, stared at him, puzzled. He saw the situation from a civilian's logic.

"It wasn't your fault. There was nothing you could do to avoid it. Why don't you just tell the truth?" the reserve officer asked.

The veteran patrolman stood staring for a moment, a perplexed expression on his face. Finally, he said, "You're right. There *wasn't* anything I could have done to avoid the accident. It just never occurred to me to tell the entire truth. The situation never came up before."

They both had a good laugh. You have to laugh when you're a cop—even if it hurts.

23

We've Come a Long Way, Baby

*T*HE CITY-COUNTY Building in Knoxville, Tennessee, sits on a high hill, the front facing Main Street, the back overlooking the Tennessee River. You can see two bridges when looking out any window from the back of the building: the Gay Street and the Henley Street bridges.

Upon those two bridges a lot of drama has been played out through the years. People wishing to make a final statement to the world sometimes jump into the swirling water below them. The drop of eighty feet or so usually is not fatal. Sometimes, if the jumper can swim, rescue occurs. Usually not, however. Most of the time it ends with a drowning, and the rescue squad dragging the river.

I have witnessed two people actually jumping from one of the bridges, several who threatened but were talked down, and I have watched dragging operations numerous times.

Once, while I was still chief of security at the City-County Building, I stood at the back window with one of my guards, Walt Minton. As we watched, Walt, who generally had little to say, made an astute comment: "If somebody had spent the money that they're spendin' to drag the river on that feller while he was alive, I bet he would never have jumped."

Walt hit the nail on the head. He was talking about priorities and the type of society which we have built. I remembered his words many years later as I once more stood looking down on the Tennessee River.

The flashing blue lights in the center of the Gay Street Bridge caught my attention as I made my way down the back hallway of the sheriff's office. Traffic on the two-lane bridge was stopped in both directions.

A man, shirtless and with hair standing wildly out from his head, was standing on one of the small platforms on the side of the bridge used by maintenance workers. Even given the distance between us, his jerky motions and agitation were clear. He was screaming at a police officer who was obviously trying to talk him down.

"What's going on?" one of the records clerks asked from behind me.

"There's a jumper on the Gay Street Bridge."

The scenario was nothing new to Stan Knight, the first officer on the scene. He had seen it many times in his career. An individual, driven off the deep end by personal demons, had climbed up to be seen and heard—or to perish.

Though I did not know who the officer was until I read it in the paper the next day, I could see that he knew what he was doing. His attitude, from my viewpoint, appeared to be one of caution and restraint.

Dealing with an irrational person is like trying to play a game in which you are not familiar with the rules. The rules exist only in the mind of the irrational person. One wrong move or gesture and the game ends without a winner.

I walked down to the parking lot and went outside so I could hear what was going on. A few people, passers-by from the parking garage, had stopped to watch curiously.

"Jump. Jump. Jump!" Several voices chanted in unison.

For the first time I saw the crowd gathered at the restaurant on the river. It is a popular place that features barbecued dishes. Close to the business district, it is the stopping point for many business luncheons and a gathering spot for affluent people on their way home for the evening.

Several people had wandered outside the building and were standing, many with drinks in hand, looking at the man above them as he teetered on the brink of a personal apocalypse. I could hear laughter from the restaurant on the banks of the river.

"Jump. Jump!" A male voice yelled. "Yes," several more joined in, "Go ahead and jump!"

The man's head swung violently to look down at the restaurant crowd. If he had expected sympathy, he got none. His plight had been reduced to an amusing spectacle.

"I will," he screamed. "I'll do it!"

"Go ahead," the voices taunted from below him. "Jump!"

As Stan Knight worked desperately to calm the man down, a police supervisor sent a cruiser down to the restaurant to stop the taunting voices.

"I can't believe this," an elderly man standing next to me said. "Those people act as if this is some kind of game. That poor man on the bridge is obviously desperate."

"Yeah," I replied. "It never ceases to amaze me. I've seen it happen before."

"Don't they believe he'll jump, or don't they care?" a woman asked.

There seemed no good answer to her question, so I said nothing.

"Good," a female voice said. "A police car just pulled into the restaurant. He'll arrest them if they don't stop yelling."

I didn't want to burst the woman's bubble, but an arrest was highly unlikely. True, what they were doing is considered disorderly conduct, but getting a conviction on such a charge would be difficult.

A good lawyer can make such a case look like hysteria on the part of an officer. I would later discover that one of Knoxville's more well-known criminal defense lawyers was among the crowd taunting the potential jumper.

We were unable to hear what the officer said to the crowd, but most of them began to disperse as the drama continued above them. By then an ambulance was standing by, along with a clergyman and a psychotherapist. The man had requested a cup of coffee, then had hurled it at Officer Knight, splattering it all over his uniform.

Such things go with the territory of being a cop. The man or woman in blue is generally the recipient of rage that cannot be directed anywhere else.

As the officer got back into his cruiser, there was a final taunt from the restaurant on the river.

"We knew you wouldn't jump!" a male voice echoed. The taunt was followed by a short, hard laugh.

By the time the man was coaxed down, through the combined efforts of clergy, therapist, and cop, the people at the restaurant had lost interest. It had become obvious that the man was not going to jump—at least not for their amusement.

Inside, they were finishing their meals and drinks as the would-be jumper was led away sobbing to an ambulance for transportation to a psychiatric ward. The diners had an amusing story to recount tomorrow.

They were not really excited, either by the jumper or the cop who had ordered them inside. If you want to see such sophisticated people upset, you must be there when they report that someone has burglarized their home or ripped the radio out of their Mercedes or BMW.

As I went back to my office that night, I thought of the man on the bridge and of the people who had dared him to jump. I was sure the man would spend a few days in lockup, then he would be back on the streets because there is not enough money available for the kind of extended therapy that most people like him need. (In fact, the man went back and actually jumped off the bridge a few months later. He was pulled alive from the waters.)

The incident stayed with me a long time. It reminded of something I had seen as a youngster. It was in a history book in the section on ancient Rome. Not the Rome of Republican days, but the Rome that came later when its citizens had traded principle for privilege.

In the picture, sleek, sophisticated people lounged back, faint smiles of amusement on their lips as they watched human beings dying on the sands of the arena. The gladiators dying on the sands obviously meant nothing to the spectators.

"We've come a long way, baby," I said to no one in particular. "A long way."

— 24 —

Things That Go Bump in the Night

*H*UMAN BEINGS LOVE to be frightened.
If not, there would be no roller coasters or ferris wheels, and Stephen King would not be one of the most well-known writers in the English-speaking world.

One of the most delicious thrills I ever experienced was while watching the movie *Psycho*. I had already figured out that Norman Bates had a split personality. I had decided, however, that his mother was merely a dummy, having missed the clues about Norman's hobby of taxidermy. When the rocking chair was swung around, revealing Mrs. Bates's mummified face, I nearly died of shock.

In their everyday lives, police officers are called on to face things never seen by most people. They deal with mangled bodies and suicides and face armed assailants. It's all in a day's work. I can tell you from experience, though, cops are just as prone to fits of imagination as civilians.

A few years ago I picked up a horror novel at a used-book store. With my family safely tucked away, I settled down to read. The book was *Salem's Lot*, Stephen King's vampire novel. Soon I was deep in the plot, sitting at the kitchen table, tensed and wide-eyed.

The rustling sound against the kitchen window caught my attention. I got up and pulled the curtain aside. There was nothing there. Soon, however, I heard it again. Finding nothing the second time, I moved myself to the living room with its thick drapes, suddenly uneasy that the gauzy kitchen curtains allowed outsiders to look in.

I was barely settled when the rustling started up again. There would be a slight clicking sound, then the rustling, persistent and loud, which echoed all the way into the living room. As the rustling and clicking continued, I was seized by a desire to go get my service revolver. It was in the bedroom, though, and I did not want to wake my wife and have her ask me why I was getting out my pistol at one in the morning.

Tip-toeing to the kitchen, I reached around and turned off the light, certain that any prowler would flee. The rustling continued. My heart began to thump as my eyes adjusted to the darkness. Easing across the kitchen, with King's vampires still fresh in my mind, I jerked open the curtain.

I recoiled in horror as large wings flapped against the pane of glass, inches from my face. Tripping over a chair, I nearly fell. Then, catching myself against the doorway, I realized with relief what I had seen.

There is a giant moth called the Luna Moth that inhabits East Tennessee. It is a lovely, pale green color and can have a wingspan of several inches. Though relatively rare, a large specimen was on my kitchen window, apparently attracted by the light.

Giggling at myself, I returned to King's novel, knowing that I would be hours settling down enough to sleep.

"It was in the cemetery. I seen it plain as day as I was comin' in from work. It was a blue light, a'dancin' in the wind."

The woman shuddered, pulling her sweater around her. A woman in her mid-fifties, she was still dressed in the white uniform of a health-care worker, which explained why she was out in the late night and early morning hours.

I decided to humor her. It is usually the easiest way to end such a call. Taking out my notepad, I stepped closer to the front door to get into the light.

"What is your full name, ma'am?"

"Why do you want my name?"

"Don't you want a report?" I asked.

"No, I *don't* want a report. I just want you to go down to the cemetery and find out what the blue light was that was floatin' around. You don't have to *humor* me. I'm not a hysterical old maid, afraid of her shadow!"

"I'll go right over there," I said, embarrassed at having been caught in the act of condescending to her.

The cemetery was within sight of the woman's house. She stood in the door as I backed out of her driveway and pulled into the cemetery. The November wind whipped leaves around in front of my headlights as I turned them off. It was not really cold, maybe fifty degrees, but I pulled on my windbreaker, picked up my flashlight, and got out of the car with a sigh. I remember thinking of the terrible injustice to police officers who must humor the public. I knew I had to make a token search for the blue light or have a complaint filed on me.

The clouds were sketchy that night, and moonlight lit the field almost like daylight, bathing it in pale yellow. The moon hung large and round in front of me. It was, I suppose, what old-timers call a "harvest moon."

I stopped dead in my tracks as a blue light floated across the face of that moon. My breathing increased as I whipped out my service revolver, thinking how useless a weapon would be against something you could see through.

Calling for back-up crossed my mind, but an officer who calls for back-up to assist in hunting for a ghostly blue light would be assured of harrassment from his fellow officers for the rest of his life. I swallowed hard and looked. Sure enough, I saw it again sparkling in the moonlight. It appeared to be about face level, a hundred or so feet ahead of me.

My mind searched for a rational explanation. Swamp gas? There was no swamp. Weather balloon? No, I had seen it clearly defined against the moon. It was not round. It was filmy, with no defined edges.

Without warning I remembered everything I had ever read about the supernatural. Visions of ectoplasmic ghosts ran through my mind, restless spirits, poltergeists, the living dead. My stomach churned as I advanced closer with each step, my weapon pointed ahead.

At a distance of twenty feet, I could see it clearly, waving pale blue in the dim light. I lifted my flashlight and thumbed it on—knees knocking together—half expecting a ghostly voice to hail me.

It was a sheet of blue, filmy plastic, the kind they wrap your suits in at the cleaners, whipping back and forth in the moonlight.

I laughed aloud—when my teeth quit chattering—and carried it back over to the complainant. She seemed as relieved as I was for the rational explanation.

Not all imaginary monsters are of the supernatural variety. I learned this one summer evening while I was still a reserve officer and answered a burglary call with a patrol officer by the name of Ron Lake.

A burglary had definitely occurred. We had found the point of entry. The question was, had the burglar left? With an audible alarm, you rarely catch the thief at the scene. The alarm we had answered, however, was "silent." The security company had called it in. We were about to enter by the door the thief had opened, when a noise came from the back of the house.

"Did you hear that?" Ron asked in a whisper.

"Yeah. You think maybe he heard us pull in and hid?"

"Maybe. Let's check. If there's still someone inside, he won't try to leave now."

Weapons in hand, we eased down the side of the house through the wet evening grass. As we stepped around to check out the back yard, there was a loud, metallic click. It sounded exactly like the safety of a shotgun being thumbed off.

Both of us dived forward at the same instant, expecting the air to be ripped by the explosion of a twelve gauge. I was desperately seeking a target, finger on trigger, when the soft flash of light came, followed by a frying sound, then a slight thump as the large insect fell to the bottom of the electronic bug killer that was hanging from a tree limb.

Without speaking, we both got up from the dew-wet lawn and proceeded to search the house. The burglar had, indeed, made his escape before we arrived. We filled out the report and headed in for the service center. It was almost quitting time.

"I thought we were dead for a moment there," Ron said, casting a glance at me as we drove down the interstate. "It sounded just like the safety of a shotgun."

"Yeah," I replied, "my knees went weak for a second."

We rode along in silence for a few minutes, then I snickered as a thought occurred to me.

"What's so funny?" he asked.

"Do you realize, if we had shot that electronic bug killer, no one would have believed why we did it? Can you imagine the kind of story we would've had to *make up?*"

He sat for a moment as it sank in, then he started laughing. We were still chuckling when we got to the service center, but we did not tell anyone what we were laughing about.

Not until now, anyway.

"Do you hear it?" the elderly man asked. He was emaciated, like a walking skeleton, and clad in a ragged, terrycloth bathrobe. His hair was thin and fluffy, standing out all over his head. He was about eighty years old and had one tooth left in front.

"Describe the sound to me," I said, putting my ear close to the kitchen sink drain.

The call had come in as "see the complainant about strange noises." Obviously agitated, the elderly man had led me directly to the kitchen.

"They're laughin' and gigglin'," he said. "It's been going on all night."

Nodding, I put my ear closer to the cracked enamel of the old sink and listened closely. I could hear the gurgling of old pipes.

"When did you first notice this?" I asked.

"Well, they've been there since the house was built in '38, but they've only become a nuisance since my wife died."

"And when did your wife die?"

"About three months ago. Can you help me?" he asked.

"What do you think is in the pipes?" I asked.

"I think we're over an Indian graveyard, and the spirits resent us a'livin' right over them," the old man said, running his fingers through his thin hair. "I *got* to get some sleep." His eyes were rimmed with red.

Moved by sudden inspiration, I opened the door under the sink. There was a box of dishwashing detergent and a can of drain cleaner.

"What are you—" the old man began to ask, but I placed my finger to my lips to signal for silence.

Stealthily, I removed the lid from the drain cleaner and poured about half of it down the sink. I waited a moment, as the old man watched with wide eyes, then turned on the water.

"That ought to do it," I said, turning off the water and putting my ear over the sink. "Yep. I hear them squealing and screaming. They won't be back for a while. I can tell you that. *Listen.*"

He leaned over and listened. Suddenly a smile crossed his face. "I hear the little devils yellin' and screamin'," he said, his single tooth fully visible. "They're gettin' further and further away!"

"That should be good for a couple of months," I told him, heading for the back door. "They can't handle the lye in the drain cleaner. Get yourself a good night's sleep."

"I appreciate it." The old man was beaming at me as he closed the door."

A social scientist may not approve of the way I handled that call, but it worked. No one was hurt, and presumably the old man was able to sleep.

It proves what I have always believed. A good cop can handle any kind of prowler.

— 25 —

Come Back When I'm Better, You Hear?

"DAVID, THIS IS Vickie Letsinger. We met at your last book signing."

"Sure," I replied, putting a face with her name. She was a pretty, blonde woman, a police officer over at Oak Ridge who had come to the bookstore with Tom Fox, a Knoxville police officer.

"I'm calling about one of our officers. His name is Don Boles. He's only thirty-four years old, and he just found out a few days ago that he has cancer. The doctors have only given him a couple of weeks to live."

Listening quietly, I felt my stomach twist. Less than three months before, I had been in the hospital for coronary by-pass surgery. That I am not immortal—that none of us is immortal—had become clear to me as the surgeon explained what they were going to do.

"Don mentioned that he had always meant to read your books, but never got around to it. We think it would mean a lot if you could come by and visit him. . . ."

"If I can't be there tomorrow, I'll make it the night after," I replied. There was no question of whether I would go, only when.

"Thanks." Vickie sounded relieved. "Randy Tedford will be working tonight if you show up. I'll be there tomorrow night. Just come to the station, and one of us will drive you to the hospital."

Randy Tedford is a big, smiling cop who is always on the verge of telling a funny story. He writes a column for the *Oak Ridger*. We met at in-service training one year and became friends.

I hung up the phone and went into the living room. Most of the time I can hide what I'm feeling, but not from my wife. She picked up instantly that something was wrong.

"Well?" she asked.

"That was Vickie Letsinger. You met her at the last book signing. She wants me to drive over to Oak Ridge and visit a cop who's dying from cancer."

"You know you're not supposed to push it. I'll drive you over there."

"No, I'll be all right."

"Just remember, you've just had major surgery."

"I know, but I'll be all right."

Sleep was a long time coming that night. The ranks of men and women in blue are thin in East Tennessee. The death of an officer leaves a big hole.

I remembered officer Verlin Littlefield that night as I tried to sleep. Cancer had done him in just short of his thirty-eighth birthday. A big bear of a man who moved with the sinewy grace of a mountain lion, Verlin had seemed indestructible until just a few short months before his death.

I first saw Verlin on Clinton Highway. Still a reserve officer then, I regarded each patrol shift as an adventure to be savored.

Lynn McBee and I had seen Verlin's cruiser parked on the lot of a nude bar that was then called Mister D's. We pulled in, planning to walk through, but Verlin came out before we got to the door.

"Not much goin' on," Verlin said.

As we paused to talk, three youngsters—college students by their dress—came out behind Verlin and walked to a new car at the edge of the lot. They were dressed much too nicely to be part of the regular working class group that normally frequents Clinton Highway.

"Oink! Oink!" one of the boys mocked as Verlin was opening his mouth to speak.

Verlin paused and turned slowly to look at the boys. They glanced at each other and grinned nervously, like little children saying naughty words in front of their parents.

"Did one of them just *oink* at me?" Verlin asked in a tone of disbelief.

"It sure sounded like it," I answered, glancing at the boys.

Slowly he turned, massive shoulders rising, with his eyebrows coming together. In no hurry, he began to walk toward the three, speaking not a word.

Two of them broke and ran down the highway almost as soon as he started his advance. The other, a tall skinny boy in a plaid shirt, was made of a little sterner stuff. He waited until the big officer was within ten feet before he broke and ran like a gazelle.

Verlin turned to us, smiling. "Go ask the manager if he wants to leave this abandoned vehicle on his lot. If he doesn't, I'll have it towed."

A smile crossed my lips as I remembered that night. Somewhere down the highway, three college boys had watched unprotesting as their car was towed away. They had learned a valuable and relatively painless lesson. They had learned why a dog cowers down in the presence of a wolf. Wolves and dogs look alike, but the dogs know the difference.

When Verlin first began to lose weight, no one paid any attention. Cops do that. They go on crash diets, lose twenty or thirty pounds, then put it back on in the slow hours when there's little to do but eat and drink coffee.

After his collapse at in-service, the end came quickly. A

few weeks is not long to live, but it is a long time to know you're dying.

Verlin's death left me almost in a state of shock. If such a mountain of a man had succumbed to death, what chance had I, a mere ordinary man?

"Hi," Vickie said. "I'm glad you could make it."

I followed her out to the cruiser and got in. She fished a copy of *Black Friday Coming Down* from beside the seat and handed it to me.

"We bought him a copy of *The Moon Is Always Full* earlier. We'd like for you to give him this one and sign the other."

"Sure," I said, swallowing hard and dreading the evening ahead. There is an unspoken belief among the general public that cops get used to death. We don't. What we do is wear masks to hide the pain that bombards us daily.

At Methodist Hospital I steeled myself as we rode up the elevator. By the time we got to Don's room, my mask was in place.

As I paused outside the door, I saw two young men by the bed. Despite their civilian clothes, I knew they were cops. Don's wife sat in a chair by the bed making small talk.

"Don, this is David Hunter," Vickie said. "He heard you were in the hospital and wanted to stop and visit a while. He brought you a copy of his other book."

His eyes were sunken and abnormally bright. Don Boles had the look of a man who has been fighting valiantly against the odds—and losing.

"It's good to meet you," he said almost in a whisper, rising from the bed to extend his hand. As I took it, he was seized by a fit of coughing. His lungs, Vickie had told me, were going quickly.

"I've been reading your book. What I've read so far is really good. I'm looking forward to finishing both of them."

My face remained expressionless only because I have had a lot of practice. I knew Don Boles would never finish either of my books, would never be thirty-five years old.

"So, how long have you been a cop, Don?"

Before he could answer, a fit of coughing seized him again.

"Ten years, and before that he was military police," one of the officers in the room said proudly.

We made small talk for a few minutes, his wife, the other two cops, and I. Don sipped water from a straw, there but not really with us. The painkillers had taken him to another place.

After a few minutes, I prepared to leave.

"Don, I have to go, but I'm glad we got to meet."

"Me, too," he said between coughs, "You come and see me when I'm well, and we'll tell some cops stories and talk about your books, you hear?"

My mask almost came off as tears burned at the back of my eyes. I swallowed hard and nodded. "We'll do that," I replied.

Outside in the hallway, I looked at Vickie questioningly.

"He was real angry the first day when they told him. Then he spent some time putting his affairs in order. Ever since, he's acted as if there's really nothing wrong."

"I hope he stays that way," I said quietly.

When Vickie called a week later, I was expecting it. It was exactly two weeks after the doctors gave their grim prophecy. Don Boles had quietly slipped away. His informal honor guard of off-duty officers was at his side when he died.

Oak Ridge is not a big department, but there was a cop with Don from the time he went in the hospital until the time they carried him out. Cops take care of their own.

The gathering at the funeral home, where we stood with badges draped in black, was not for Don Boles. He was already beyond the sufferings of this world. It was to comfort those of us left behind.

We remembered a man who went out daily and put his body between evil and innocence, between the weak and the helpless and those who would do them harm.

A good cop's life is testimony to principle. There are no paper tigers or parlor warriors working the streets. Like every good cop, Don Boles daily proclaimed his belief in the law by putting up his life for collateral.

We'll remember him at roll call.

— 26 —

A Routine Patrol Call

I LISTENED QUIETLY as the dispatcher gave out a call to the north units. It was a family dispute, and shots had been fired. The object of the disturbance had locked himself inside his trailer and had sent his family away. He was armed with a rifle and a shotgun.

Tim Collins of Adam Detachment responded that he was on the way. His back-up unit warned him that she was coming from a fairly long distance.

"Unit 10, I'm close. I'll back the patrol unit up," I radioed.

"Ten-four, Unit 10," the dispatcher acknowledged me.

At that time it was not my job to answer patrol calls. I investigated and inspected places that sell beer. I have never ceased being a street cop in my heart, though.

The location of the disturbance was way out in the country, almost on the county line, a long way from back-up. Deputy sheriffs who work rural beats learn early that the help you have upon arrival at the scene is the only help you'll have if things get messy.

Dropping off into a valley and through a tree-lined street that had the appearance of a tunnel as my headlights plunged ahead of me, I tried to tell the dispatcher that I was almost there.

The radio beeped quietly, telling me that my transmission had not hit the repeater. At that moment I met Collins at an intersection and fell in behind him.

Driving up another ridge, we saw several people standing in a yard beside a small frame house. They had the frightened look of people confronted with a situation they could not comprehend, let alone control.

We killed the lights and got out of our cruisers. I listened as Collins elicited what information he could get from the distraught family members.

As he was talking to them, I opened the trunk of my cruiser, took out my soft body armor, and began to pull it on. My actions were not lost on the family. Eyes widened as I removed my Mossberg twelve-gauge pump and racked in a round.

Patrol officers wear body armor all the time. It is required. With investigators and detectives, it is optional. Each plain-clothes officer weighs the odds of a shoot-out against the discomfort of wearing the armor. Comfort usually wins out.

When you wear the armor every day, it becomes a part of the uniform, like your weapon and your badge. It is a different matter entirely when you put it on at the scene. You become sharply aware of *why* you have put it on. It is because you have reason to expect that someone is going to try to kill you within the next few minutes.

The story was not an unfamiliar one. The man had been experiencing personal problems, which he had tried to solve with ever-increasing doses of alcohol. A Vietnam veteran, he had not been the same since returning home.

Tonight he had staggered through his home, drunk and belligerent, ordering his wife and children out. After they fled, a shot had rung out. They did not know if he had shot himself or if he had merely fired at random.

It would be our job to find out what had happened.

As Tim and I started up the long driveway, a third cruiser arrived. Stopping for a moment, Tim told the officer to cover the front door in case the man decided to bolt out when we approached. He assumed, of course, that the man was still alive and not lying on the carpet with his brains leaking out.

There was no need for conversation as Tim and I made our way up the driveway, taking what cover we could in the shadows. We go back a long way. We were jailers together, and I had absolute confidence that he would be there if things went bad. We had covered each other before.

A chunky individual in his thirties, Collins is a man of few words. When he does speak, however, he is blunt and to the point. Once I overheard him talking to a defense lawyer. As I approached, I caught the tail end of the conversation.

"You do see what I'm getting at, don't you?" The lawyer was obviously under the impression that he was dealing with a man willing to play word games. He was young and new to the Knox County courts, or he would have known better.

"Yeah, I understand," Collins said. "You want me to act like your dirt-bag client didn't get drunk and drive down a crowded highway. Right?"

The lawyer found himself at a loss for words.

We darted across the driveway, exposing ourselves to possible gunfire, to reach the end of the trailer. Standing on our toes, we tried to look inside. We could see nothing.

With Tim in the lead, I followed, shotgun at the ready. It was loaded, but with the safety still on. We moved quietly, hugging the side of the trailer and being careful not to let our heads silhouette against a window.

Out of the darkness, a horrible snarling hurtled toward us. Whirling, we saw a dark shape and heard the sound of a dog chain unwinding. A large, snarling dog made for us as fast as he could run.

I swung the shotgun toward him, thumbing the safety off. Suddenly, just as I began to squeeze the trigger, the dog hit the end of his chain, rearing up in rage and foaming at the mouth. He was about ten feet from us when the chain caught him.

"So much for the element of surprise," I muttered under my breath.

Tim ran past the door, jerking it open as he passed, then whirled to crouch on the other side, pistol drawn. The barrel of my shotgun was covering the open door. I could see into the back bedroom, and Collins could see down the hallway.

"John [not his real name], we need to talk to you. This is the Knox County Sheriff's Department," Collins called out.

There was silence from inside as the big dog continued to hurl himself at the end of the chain, filling the air with canine indignation. I glanced at the dog, wondering how much punishment the chain could take.

Tim nodded at me. Rising in unison, we "button-hooked" through the door. I now faced the long hallway leading to the kitchen and living room, and he faced the back bedroom. A moment later he had checked the room, and we moved down the long hallway.

"I hear him breathing," Tim whispered.

We both eased up to the bar that separated the kitchen from the living room and peeked over quickly. The man was supine on the couch, a rifle and shotgun across his chest.

He was either passed out, or he wanted us to think he was.

Nodding again, I stepped around the counter and aimed the shotgun directly at the man's head. My heart was trying to pound out of its cavity, and my breathing was labored.

A pistol can be a defensive weapon; a police shotgun is for shooting people at close range. It is the most deadly weapon in the street cop's arsenal. When you have the shotgun in your hand, you are expecting a deadly confrontation.

The man did not move as I stood ready to shoot him.

Tim crossed the room in one quick movement and snatched both weapons away from him. A kitchen knife was stuck into the couch above him, and there were superficial cuts on his wrists, but nothing serious.

We both began to breathe deeply, each ignoring the other's obvious tension and relief. Tim opened the front door and gave a thumbs-up to the patrol officer outside.

The radio would not work, so I picked up the phone and dialed E-911 to tell them we were safe and would be back on the air shortly.

Back at the car, I took off my body armor and removed the live round from my shotgun as Tim talked to the man's family. Their story rang familiar. There are a lot of disturbed people out there, and cops eventually meet most of them.

The family did not want the man taken away; the danger had been removed. They said he would not harm anyone on purpose, but promised to get him some help "tomorrow."

I looked at Collins and shrugged. We had seen no crime committed. He warned them that the situation could become worse, then got in his car, perfectly aware that his advice probably had fallen on deaf ears.

After all, if there was trouble again, the cops would come and put their lives on the line once more. Cops are used to violence, you know. It doesn't bother them, does it? It's their job to clean up messes and take risks.

As we drove away that night down the long gravel drive, tremors ran through my stomach as the tension began to leave. I was glad to be alive. After a while, you forget what it feels like to enter a place where death may be waiting.

It was not unusual for a patrol call. Some might call it routine—some civilians that is. Cops know there are no routine calls.

In the movies, the SWAT team would have come out in black fatigues to handle the situation. In real life on a rural beat, if you called for special help every time you were confronted with danger, there'd be no one to work the beat.

I was glad to help that night, but glad also to be going home. The patrol officers might very well have another such call in the next few hours.

It reminded me of something all cops ought to remember. Patrol is the backbone of any police department. The rest of us just back them up. Sometimes we need to thank them and let them know we appreciate what they do. It's important. I know because I've been there.

Of course, they'll go on doing it whether you say thanks or not.

— 27 —

The Best-laid Plans of Mice and Men

*I*F NARCOTICS OFFICERS had their way, all drug deals would be made in open fields. That way, if the deal goes sour they are far from civilization; the only people at the scene are criminals and cops.

Drug dealers know this. They know that cops worry about hurting innocent people, and so they prefer to set up their deals in highly populated, high traffic areas.

This particular operation was like many others. The dealer had been "set up" by a woman who knew him. He was to meet a man who had been presented to him as a street dealer who would buy several ounces of cocaine. In real life the street dealer was Officer Jimmy Jones, a Knox County officer assigned to the Metro Narcotics Unit.

Known to friends as "J. J.," Jimmy is a pleasant, middle-class young man who is able to take on the coloration of the underworld very successfully. Legend has it that one suspect who hoped to buy drugs took one look at Jimmy (who was posing as a dealer) and refused to do business with anyone who looked so thoroughly disreputable.

The meeting had been set up in a parking lot of a national restaurant chain. Since the sting was taking place in the evening hours, six teams of officers—a total of fourteen—were involved in the operation. These officers also had five vehicles, which were to converge on the suspect's vehicle and block it in when Jimmy gave the word. Jimmy was wired with a transmitter so that everyone in on the drug bust could hear what was being said.

At first, everything moved smoothly. The dealer [we'll call him Carl] arrived with two associates. One of them made contact by walking across the parking lot to Jimmy's vehicle. The informant, who was riding with Jimmy, went to the suspect's vehicle to verify the cocaine. Once there, she climbed into Carl's vehicle for less than a minute, got back out, and returned with Carl's confederate to J. J.'s car to get the money.

Jimmy saw immediately that his informant was terrified, but he didn't know that her terror was caused by what she had seen in the vehicle: a "machine gun," other handguns, and grenades. It turned out that they were smoke grenades, but she didn't know it.

Back at Jimmy's vehicle, Carl's associate leaned in and told him to "be cool." The people they were doing business with were "real paranoid," he warned. When the informant looked at Jimmy in terror as she reached for the money, he told her to take the cash to Carl and "everything will be all right."

The informant and dealer were halfway between Jimmy's car and Carl's, when the officer gave the word over his body mike for all units to converge and arrest the suspects. It was at this point that the plan began to unravel.

Carl immediately grasped the situation and floored the accelerator of his car, striking two officers and his colleague who was returning to his car with the informant. As Carl swung his vehicle around, attempting to escape, the second associate either fell or was thrown out of the car and was quickly taken into custody.

Jimmy Jones and other officers began firing their weap-

ons in an attempt to disable Carl's vehicle. Despite all pre-
cautions, however, Carl was able to drive around the
officers and flee southbound, two police undercover vehicles in hot pursuit.

While the suspect was being chased, the informant managed to tell Jones about the weapons and grenades. Believ-
ing that one of the weapons was fully automatic and that the
grenades were of the fragmentation type, he quickly radioed the information to the officers in pursuit.

When Carl turned west onto one of Knoxville's most
heavily traveled thoroughfares, police vehicles followed in
close pursuit. Officer Nevil Norman of the Knox County
Sheriff's Department succeeded in passing the suspect's vehicle, despite his attempts to run Norman off the road by
sideswiping him. Working in unison, the officers began to
slow the drug dealer's progress by reducing their speed.

By this time, patrol units of the sheriff's department had
been alerted and were moving toward the dealer, which Carl
surely realized. Without warning, he swerved across the
four-lane road into a small shopping center. Apparently he
was attempting to go eastbound again. He never left the
parking lot, however, apparently choosing to shoot it out
before more officers arrived rather than surrender.

As Carl turned inside the vehicle, he pointed a weapon
out of the window. Officer Norman fired at the vehicle's
tires, trying to disable it, and Officer Jay Witt of the Knoxville Police Department fired two rounds from his service
revolver. The suspect slumped over the wheel with a bullet
wound in his neck.

Even then, the incident was not over. Carl's vehicle rolled
from the parking lot and struck another vehicle head on.
Within minutes, Knox County patrolman Larry Hunter arrived, checked the injured parties in the vehicle that had
been struck, reassured them that an ambulance was on the
way, then ran to Carl's vehicle where several officers were
then standing.

In the vehicle, Hunter saw the suspect slumped over, a

revolver near his hand and what appeared to be an automatic weapon and an extra clip beside him. Carl's drug
dealing days were over—he was totally paralyzed from the
neck wound.

The incident, which took only minutes to transpire, gen-
erated hundreds of pages of testimony.

Many years ago, the poet Robert Burns cut into
a nest of mice as he plowed a field. After watching the mice
scatter, he wrote a poem that described how the "best laid
plans of mice and men" are subject to outside force. In no
area of human endeavor is this more true than in police
work, as was illustrated when the Metro Narcotics Unit
tried to bust up a drug ring one evening in late December
1987.

And Carl? Well, a suit was filed on his behalf alleging
that the officers used excessive force. I'm happy to report
that the suit came to nothing.

— 28 —

A Monster in the Stairwell

*T*HERE WAS A MONSTER lurking in the stairwell, under the bright orange roof of the Howard Johnson's Motor Lodge in Greensboro, North Carolina, on a warm July evening in 1989. Before the night was over, he would test my limits as a police officer and a human being.

It just happened to be a Howard Johnson's. The first motel at that exit had been full. The management could not have prevented the incident because monsters look like ordinary people. "Clean-cut and well-groomed," my wife would later describe the man.

It had been a good week. In Spartanburg and Greenville, South Carolina, I had appeared on television, done two radio talk shows, and signed books. In addition, it was the closest thing we would have to a family vacation that year.

My son, Paris, then eight, and my daughter Elaine, fourteen, were looking forward to visiting relatives in Charlotte after the last day of the tour. However, I had a television show scheduled in Greensboro and a newspaper interview in Winston-Salem first.

Arriving in Greensboro around ten in the evening, we

first located the television station so I would have no trouble at seven the next morning. I am barely functional early in the day. Everything must be laid out for me.

After assuring myself that I could locate the station even in the early hours, we drove back over to the interstate to find a place to stay. The first place of lodging off the ramp had no vacancies. Across the road, we checked into Howard Johnson's.

Our room was on the second floor, up one flight of stairs. We carried a load of things up, checked out the room, and had the kids start getting ready for bed because it was after eleven by that time.

"I'm going down to get another load," I said.

"I'll be right behind you," Cheryl told me.

Behind the rented Ford, I paused to stretch and breathe in the comfortable North Carolina air, highly pleased with myself and with my lot in life. My first book, *The Moon Is Always Full*, was gaining critical success, even if we had not made the *New York Times* bestseller list.

It felt good to be in a place where I would not be asked to intervene in the affairs of other people, where I would not have to enforce the law. A cop never really relaxes unless he is far removed from his jurisdiction. There are a lot of people out there with grudges to settle, and you never know when you'll run into them.

As I opened the trunk, a drama was being played out less than twenty feet from me, behind the walls of the motel. . . .

"Don't open this door for anyone," Cheryl told Paris and Elaine. "I'm going down to help your father. We'll be right back."

A brown-eyed beauty of Spanish descent, Cheryl turns heads. Beauty was not the trait that brought her in contact with the monster, though. She was simply in an empty hallway where a monster was lurking.

He was standing between her and the stairwell door, and

she paused, not really alarmed. At first glance, he seemed harmless. Then he began to walk toward her.

"Everything's all right," he said quietly. Cheryl did not react until he reached for her.

"Don't!" she screamed, knocking his hands away.

"Everything's *all right*," he said, reaching again.

Once more she knocked his hands away and ran back to the door. "Call the operator, Elaine," Cheryl yelled. "Tell them to send the police!"

The man did not flee but stood calmly, "like he was waiting to see if there was *really* anyone else in the room," Cheryl would later tell me.

Hearing Elaine's response, he turned calmly and went through the stairwell door. Cheryl could see me below through the motel window, but she was afraid to enter the stairwell until the man emerged into view.

Downstairs, I was setting items on the ground, waiting for Cheryl to come and help me. I saw the man walk out the stairwell door, but took no note of him.

Had he run out, I might have pursued out of habit. Had he been excited, I would have noticed because cops are alert to things like that. There was nothing out of the ordinary about him. He was merely a neatly dressed, slender man with neatly trimmed hair.

He was about fifty feet away when Cheryl emerged from the door and pointed at him. "David, that man tried to attack me!"

At that point the man ran toward a light blue car, and I reached for my service revolver instinctively. It was, of course, in the car because I was out of my jurisdiction, but it took me only an instant to grab it.

I pounded down the sidewalk after him, but he had gotten into the car and fired up the engine. Increasing my speed, I cut across the grass, hoping to intersect with him at the edge of the building.

Moments later, I saw that I was not going to make it.

Tires were squealling under the pale blue car, and events were moving so fast that I could not even identify the make.

The urge to empty my revolver through the rear window was almost overpowering. Mediocre marksman that I am, I knew I could hit him. Maybe not with every round, but enough to stop him.

Fortunately, even through the red haze of rage that possessed me, ten years of police training asserted itself. You do not fire at a fleeing suspect unless a life-threatening situation is imminent. You most assuredly do not fire in a crowded area where innocent people may be injured.

As the blue car whipped around the building, I charged into the motel office, sweating and red in the face, with weapon in hand. The clerk went white and stepped back.

"Call the police!" I gasped. "Tell them an officer needs assistance. Do it now!" I commanded, slapping my badge case down on the counter.

"I . . . just called them. A woman called from one of the rooms. The dispatcher said there was a car close. They're probably here by now." He stared, as if fascinated by my Smith & Wesson two-inch revolver.

"Thanks," I told him, somewhat embarrassed by my unprofessional behavior. I had a lot of experience at being a cop, but almost none as a victim.

By the time I walked back, exhausted from the adrenalin rush, a competent-looking police officer was interviewing my wife in the hallway outside the room. His eyebrows went up as he saw the weapon in my hand. I opened my badge case, and he nodded.

"Did you get a tag number?" he asked me.

"No, I didn't get close enough."

"Excuse me." A blonde woman of middle age emerged from a room. "Are you here about a man prowling the hallway?"

"Yes," the officer replied. "Do you know anything about it?"

"Well, a clean-cut man tried to push me into a corner a

while ago, but when I pushed him away, he left. I think he's staying on this floor somewhere."

I concealed my rage. If the woman had reported the earlier incident, my wife might not have been his second intended victim of the evening.

"He had the locks on all the stairwell doors wedged open with paper," the officer told me. "I found this at the other end of the building." He extended several wedges of folded paper.

"The doors weren't locked. He just wanted to be able to have his hands free so he could kick the doors open with his feet," I said to the officer.

A chill went up my spine. Cheryl had almost become a casualty, not of chance encounter but of a monster who calmly wedged open stairwell doors so he would have his hands free to drag a victim into a stairwell.

The officer finished his report, and we walked outside.

"He's registered here," I said.

"I know," the officer answered, watching me and waiting.

"But you have no probable cause to knock on doors at random."

"Right." He looked sympathetic.

"And he does this a lot. He has it down pat. This guy knows how small the chances are of being caught. He just waits until he finds a woman who freezes, then enjoys himself."

"You're probably right," the officer nodded. "I'll check with the clerk, but they just changed shifts. With all the people here, I doubt that the clerk will remember an ordinary looking man like your wife and the other lady described. He's probably parked somewhere watching us. When I'm gone, he'll go back to his room and probably clear out early."

We stood quietly for a moment.

"If we were in your jurisdiction, what would you tell the husband of a victim?" he asked me.

"To go to his room and let the police handle the matter."

"Right." He replied.

I nodded and opened the trunk of my car. Reaching in, I took out one of my books and autographed it for the officer. We shook hands, and he started back to his cruiser.

"I'll be close the rest of the night." He waved as he was leaving. It was a short, snappy wave that cops give each other, a lift of the hand that stops just short of a being a military salute. I have seen it among cops in every jurisdiction I ever visited.

I went back to the room, rage turning to depression. If the man was caught, all we had was a simple case of assault and battery, at the most. We knew what he had intended, and the police officer knew what he had intended, but you can't convict people, not even monsters, of intent.

The next morning, after I left for the television station, Cheryl walked out on the balcony. As she stood there, the man emerged from the building below and walked away carrying a suitcase.

There was nothing she could do but watch an ordinary looking man get into a pale blue car, which he had parked a few hundred yards away. To see him, no one would ever suspect that he was a monster by night, lurking in stairwells and looking for a victim.

Monsters are like that. They don't wear signs. They simply get their perverted desires down to a routine, secure in the knowledge that they will probably not be caught. No one knows better than a rapist how many sexual assaults are never reported by victims too traumatized even to talk about the experience of being violated.

Cheryl can now walk down a hallway without panic. For months afterward, she could not do that. It only takes a momentary brush with a monster to change your life forever.

My wife now carries a stun gun that I bought her. Her daily walks through the underground parking lot where she works always reminds her of that night in Greensboro under Howard Johnson's bright orange roof.

She'll never quite feel secure again, and neither will I. Even my own wife, twenty feet away from me, was not safe. There is no haven secure enough to keep out monsters.

There was one benefit, though. When I question a victim now, I'm a little gentler, a little better cop for the experience. I was aware, perhaps for the first time, that my badge is no magic talisman. It does not give my family immunity from the dangers out there.

Now I understand at a gut level what I only knew in my mind. After an encounter with a monster, things are never quite the same.

— 29 —

Just People Helping People

*T*HE WOMAN, STRANDS of hair plastered to her face where the tears had streaked her wind-roughened complexion, sat sobbing at a back corner booth. She was an old twenty-five or a young thirty-five. That her life had not been an easy one could be discerned by her clean but shabby clothes.

Two little girls, four or five years old, with flaxen hair, sat and watched their mother with tense, frightened looks. I saw a flash of fear cross the older child's eyes as I approached.

"Daddy left us," she blurted out. "He just put our stuff out of the car while we was in the bathroom and left us!"

One of the waitresses had called the Knox County Sheriff's Department after becoming concerned with the woman's weeping. I had been dispatched to check on her and the little girls.

"Is that so, little lady?" I asked the other child, who merely nodded, eyes growing large as saucers.

"I want the two of you to climb up on those stools over there and order something to eat. They have hot dogs, hamburgers, and all kinds of good stuff. You can see your mommy from over there."

Reluctantly they crossed to the stools, watching over their shoulders. I held up a menu and signaled the waitress to take their order.

"Now, what's the problem?" I asked.

"Just what my little one said. My husband just drove off and left us." She wiped her eyes with the back of her hand.

"I see," was my somewhat lame reply.

"No, it ain't what you think. He's not a cruel man—just a man at the end of his rope. He's been out of work for a year. We were flat broke, and he figured we'd get more help alone than if he stayed. He's been saying that for days." She broke into fresh sobbing.

"Do you have family?" I asked.

"The nearest is in Chicago," she replied.

I explained to her that there were agencies to help her along the way. We sat there discussing it as she pulled herself together.

When the waitress brought hot dogs and french fries to the little girls, I went to the counter and ordered the woman a cup of coffee. Taking out my wallet, I extended money for the food. The litle girls went at the hot dogs as if they had not eaten in a while.

"The boss says 'no charge' for the food," the waitress said. "We know what's going on but didn't know what to do. We saw her stand outside and look down the interstate after he drove off. Then she came in here and started to cry."

I carried the coffee to the table and set it in front of her. She quietly stirred in sugar and cream and began to sip it slowly, tears still brimming her eyes.

"Officer, excuse me."

A big man in jeans, T-shirt, and a baseball cap stood by the counter. I got up and went to see what he wanted. I suddenly noticed that the normal buzz of conversation was absent and that the patrons, most of them long-distance truck drivers, sat staring in our direction.

"Here," he said, extending a handful of bills. "The waitress told us what was going on. We passed the hat. There ought to be enough here to get the woman and her little girls started on their way."

"I'm sure she'll appreciate it," I said. "Can I tell her your name?"

"Nope," he raised his hands and backed away as if embarrassed. "Just see that she gets the money. Tell her it was from folks with families of their own. And . . . wish her good luck, will you?"

The patrons of the restaurant had raised enough money to buy bus tickets to Chicago and to feed the woman and little girls along the way. When I handed the money to the woman, she began to sob again.

Before I could offer to drive her and the children to the bus station, a couple with two children of their own came to the table. The woman slid in and put her arm around the sobbing mother to offer comfort.

I backed away from the situation and called my dispatcher on the radio to tell her that no police action would be required. The situation had been resolved.

There was a smile on my face as I left the truck stop. A police officer sees the worst in people most of the time. It is gratifying to be reminded that kindness and love exist out there.

People helping people—the ancient words of a Galilean rabbi echoing through the centuries and becoming reality at a truckstop in East Tennessee: "Therefore all things whatsoever ye would that men should do to you, do ye even so to them. . . ." Amen.

Epilogue

AND SO WE COME to the end of another book.

But it isn't really an ending, is it? There are no real endings when you are dealing with flesh and blood people, only pauses. There is a morning after, a time when we look back at what we've done then look ahead to what we wish to do in the future.

A thousand years ago I might have gathered at a long, wooden table to listen to my fellow warriors recount their deeds in epic poems. In this plastic and stainless steel society of ours, the warriors have all but gone mute when it comes to discussing their exploits in public. I try to fill that gap.

We no longer gather at the long table to drink mead and spin tales. Instead, we gather before roll call in the evening, sitting in chrome and plastic chairs or in the morning at the service center by the gasoline pumps, to update each other about what happened the night before—a loud and sometimes profane group.

There is never a lack of material. Time goes on. The bad guys we locked away five years ago are back on the streets, ready to match wits and do battle again.

Not long ago, a talk show hostess asked me why there is such an intense interest in police officers. Feeling a little silly but not knowing what else to say except what I believe, I told her that police officers are the last warriors who confront the enemy one on one, face to face.

It has been said that World War I was the last war fought primarily by men and that all other wars since have consisted mainly of machine against machine. For the most part, modern soldiers are miles apart during battle. The resulting deaths are no less horrible for it, but there is a lack of *personal* drama to such fighting.

Not so with the police officer. Every encounter is personal. In most cases of police combat, a lone officer takes on an assailant. Forty percent of the time, there is more than one opponent. Around a hundred times a year, officers die at the hands of their assailants.

It is an ongoing passion play, an eternal drama.

And even as I finish this collection of stories, the notes for the next collection are on my desk.

So this is but a pause, not an ending.